Access 2002

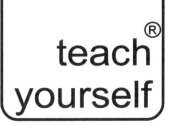

# Access 2002

## moira stephen

For UK orders: please contact Bookpoint Ltd., 130 Milton Park, Abingdon, Oxon OX14 4SB. Telephone: +44 (0)/1235 827720. Fax: +44 (0)/1235 400454. Lines are open 09.00–18.00, Monday to Saturday, with a 24-hour message answering service. You can also order through our website www.madaboutbooks.com.

For USA order enquiries: please contact McGraw-Hill Customer Services, PO Box 545, Blacklick, OH 43004-0545, USA. Telephone: 1-800-722-4726. Fax: 1-614-755-5645.

For Canada order enquiries: please contact McGraw-Hill Ryerson Ltd., 300 Water St, Whitby, Ontario L1N 9B6, Canada. Telephone: 905 430 5000. Fax: 905 430 5020.

Long renowned as the authoritative source for self-guided learning – with more than 30 million copies sold worldwide – the *Teach Yourself* series includes over 300 titles in the fields of languages, crafts, hobbies, business, computing and education.

*British Library Cataloguing in Publication Data*
A catalogue record for this title is available from The British Library.

*Library of Congress Catalog Card Number:* On file.

First published in UK 2003 by Hodder Headline Plc., 338 Euston Road, London, NW1 3BH.

First published in US 2003 by Contemporary Books, A Division of The McGraw-Hill Companies,
1 Prudential Plaza, 130 East Randolph Street, Chicago, Illinois 60601 USA.

 Typeset by MacDesign, Southampton
Printed in Great Britain for Hodder & Stoughton Educational, a division of Hodder Headline Plc, 338 Euston Road, London NW1 3BH by Cox & Wyman Ltd., Reading, Berkshire.

Impression number    10 9 8 7 6 5 4 3 2 1

Year                           2007 2006 2005 2004 2003

contents

# preface

This book is for the user who wants to be able to harness the power of Access *without* being overpowered by database jargon and difficult concepts. Whether you have never used a database in your life, or are familiar with databases but new to Access, this book will have you quickly up and running on this very popular package.

By using examples that are familiar to us all, this book takes you through the main processes that will help you build and use efficient Access databases. You can either work from beginning to end (recommended for new users) or dip into any chapter that interests you and apply the techniques to your own database.

* **Database design**: What do you want from your database? What data will you need to store? How can you organize your data efficiently in a database? These areas are explored to help you develop and design your databases.

* **Jargon and concepts**: Jargon and new concepts are explained in layman's terms – you won't be bombarded with computer-speak!

* **Essential database skills**: Setting up table structures, entering and editing data and extracting data from your database are all explored in this book.

* **Ease of use**: Whether you are designing a database for your own use, or one for others to use, the interface between you and the data is very important. You will

find out how to design friendly 'front-ends' for your databases, so that once a database is set up, it is easy to use.

- **Efficient working practices:** Finally, **macros** are introduced to give you an insight into how they can help you become more efficient as you use Access.

This book will be a useful teaching and learning aid, whether you are working by yourself or teaching others in a classroom situation. The fact that the book contains a main project that can be worked through makes it ideal teaching material.

I hope you enjoy *Teach Yourself Access 2002*, and have success in working with your databases.

Moira Stephen

September 2002

# 01

# getting started

**In this unit you will learn**

- what you need to run Access 2002
- how to install the software
- how to start Access
- about the Access screen and its tools
- how to use the Help system

## Aims of this chapter

This chapter introduces you to the Access relational database management system (RDBMS). It explains the concept of an RDBMS and demystifies some jargon. It gives an overview of the system requirements and installation procedure. It highlights the need to plan and prepare your data, to help ensure that you get maximum benefit from using Access. It also discusses the on-line Help system.

# 1.1 What is a database?

A database is simply a collection of data. For example, it may be your Christmas card name and address list, or details about books, CDs and videos in your library or it may be company data (with details of customers, suppliers, products sold, orders, employees). The data is *collected* and *organized* for a particular purpose.

Most modern database management systems (including Access) use the *relational* database management model. This simply means that all the data stored in the database is related to one subject, e.g. your company, or the items in your library.

In a simple database, it may be feasible to store all the information together in one table (see section 1.2 for a definition if necessary) – for instance, a Christmas card name and address list. Other databases are more complex – your library or company database for example. The data would then need to be divided up into several tables, which could be linked as and when required. Data about two classes of information (such as 'books' and 'publishers' in a library situation) can be manipulated as a single entry based on related data values.

For example, in your library you might want to store specific details on each book – title, author, category, ISBN, number held, year published, publisher, etc. – on your system. It would be very repetitive (and pointless) to store all the name, address and other contact details for the publisher with each book detail, since you may have the same detail duplicated hundreds of times, if one publisher is responsible for many of your books.

Therefore, in a relational system, when you store information about a book, you include a data field that can be used to connect each book with its publisher details, e.g. *Publisher Code*. The publisher details would then be stored in a separate table. The name, address and contact details of each publisher would only need to be recorded once, and could be linked to any book through the *Publisher Code* field whenever necessary.

# 1.2 Database jargon

Some database terminology may be unfamiliar to you. Below you will find brief definitions of the terms you are likely to meet in the near future. Don't worry about trying to understand them all at once – things become clearer as you use Access.

### Table

In a relational database, all the data on one topic is stored in a *table*. If your database requirements are fairly simple, you might have only one table in your database. If your requirements are more complex, your database may contain several tables. In the Library database example, you could have a table for your book data, one for your publisher data and perhaps one for author data.

The data in the table is structured in a way that will allow you to interrogate the data when and as required. All of the data on one item, e.g. a book or a publisher, is held in the *record* for that book or publisher, within the appropriate table.

### Record

A *record* contains information about a single item in your table. All the detail relating to one book will be held in that book's record in the Book table. Information about a publisher will be held in a record for that publisher in the Publisher table. The record is broken down into several *fields* – one for each piece of detail about your item (book, publisher, etc.).

### Field

A *field* is a piece of data within a record. In your book's record, things like book title, author-firstname, author-surname, category, number held, library code, location, ISBN, publisher code, etc. would all be held in separate fields. In a publisher record, you would have fields for name, address (perhaps separate fields for street, town, postcode, county), telephone number, fax number, e-mail address, etc.

Each field has a name that identifies it.

### Relationship

This determines the way in which the detail in one table is related to the detail in another table, e.g. through the publisher code. Publishers would have a *one-to-many* relationship with books as one publisher could have published many books.

### Join

The process of linking tables or queries.

### Data definition

The process of defining what data will be stored in your database, specifying the data field's type (it might be numbers or characters), the data field's size and indicating how it is related to data in other tables.

### Data manipulation

Once your data is set up, you can work with it in many ways – this may involve sorting it into a specific order, extracting specific records from tables, or listing detail from a number of different tables into one report.

# 1.3  Schematic diagram

The diagram opposite illustrates a simple database. The *Book* table would be related to the *Publisher* table through the publisher code field. The *Book* table has been expanded to indicate what fields might be included in it. In the example, the *Author* table could be related to both the *Publisher* table and the *Book* table.

* Each *record* in a table is presented in a *row* – in this example each book is a record.
* Each *field* in a table is in a *column* – there is a *Title* field, *Author* field, etc.
* Each field has a *field name* at the top of the column – *Title*, *Author*, *Category*.

**Example of a Library Database**

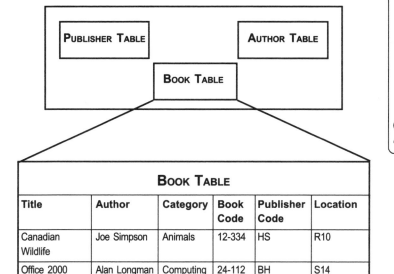

| BOOK TABLE | | | | | |
|---|---|---|---|---|---|
| Title | Author | Category | Book Code | Publisher Code | Location |
| Canadian Wildlife | Joe Simpson | Animals | 12-334 | HS | R10 |
| Office 2000 | Alan Longman | Computing | 24-112 | BH | S14 |
| Cooking with Herbs | Ann Anderson | Nutrition | 10-312 | AB | A10 |
| Hiking in Iceland | Thomas Allan | Travel | 20-100 | XY | B17 |

# 1.4 Access Objects

An Access database consists of *objects* that can be used to input, display, interrogate, print and automate your work. They are listed in the *Database* window. The purpose of each object is summarized below.

**Tables** 🔲 Tables

Tables are the most important objects in your database. Tables are used for data entry and edit.

In a table, each record is displayed as a row and each field is displayed as a column. You can display a number of records on the screen at any one time, and as many fields as will fit on your screen. Any records or fields not displayed can be scrolled into view as required.

## Queries `⊟ Queries`

You use Queries to locate specific records within your tables. You might want to extract records that meet specific selection criteria (e.g. all employees on Grade G in the accounts department). When you run a Query, the results are arranged in columns and rows like a table.

## Forms `⊞ Forms`

You can use Forms to provide an alternative to tables for data entry and viewing records. With Forms, you arrange the fields as required on the screen – you can design your forms to look like the printed forms (invoices, order forms, etc.) that you use.

When you use Forms, you display one record at a time on your screen.

## Reports `⊞ Reports`

Reports can be used to produce various printed outputs from data in your database. Using Reports, the same database can produce, for instance, a list of one publisher's books, a set of mailing labels for your letters, or a report on books in a specific category.

## Data Access Pages `⊡ Pages`

You can view and manipulate data from an Access database on an intranet or the Internet using a data access page. Data Access Pages can be used for data entry (perhaps to collect orders from customers), interactive reporting (publishing summaries of data held in the database) or data analysis.

## Macros and Modules `⊟ Macros`  `⊗ Modules`

Macros and Modules are used to automate the way you use Access, and can be used to build some very sophisticated applications. They are introduced at the end of this book.

# 1.5 Hardware and software requirements

The hardware and software specifications given are for Office XP.

The recommended configuration is a PC with Windows 2000 or XP, a Pentium processor and 128 Mb of RAM.

The minimum specification is as follows:

| Personal computer | Pentium 133 MHz or higher processor |
|---|---|
| Operating system | Windows 98, Windows Me, Windows NT 4.0 with Service Pack 6 or later, Windows 2000, or Windows XP. |
| RAM | Depends on the operating system used, plus 8Mb for each office application in use at one time.<br>**Windows 98**: 24 Mb of RAM<br>**Windows Me or NT**: 32 Mb of RAM<br>**Windows 2000 or XP**: 64 Mb of RAM |
| Hard disk | Approximately 245 Mb of hard disk space in total, with 115 Mb on the hard disk where the operating system is installed. |
| CD-ROM drive | The software is only supplied on CD |
| Monitor | Super VGA or higher-resolution |
| Mouse | Microsoft Mouse, IntelliMouse® or compatible pointing device |

See **http://www.microsoft.com/uk/office/evaluation/ sysreqs.asp** for full details of system requirements.

# 1.6 Installing Access

If you have bought a new computer at the same time as the software, the software is most probably pre-installed on your hard disk. If this is the case you can skip this bit.

Access is available as a stand-alone package and in the following versions of Microsoft Office XP:

* **Professional**: Access, Excel, Outlook, PowerPoint, Word.

* **Premium**: As professional, FrontPage, Sharepoint Team Services, Developer tools.

* **Professional with Publisher**: (only available pre-installed)

The instructions for installing Microsoft Office are:

1 Insert Disk 1 into the CD-ROM drive.

2 Follow the instructions on your screen.

3 Repeat the process for the other disks.

# 1.7 Preparing your data

The most important (and often difficult) stage in setting up any database takes place away from the computer. Before you set up a database you must get your data organized.

There are two key questions that need to be addressed:

• What do I want to store?

• What information do I want to get out of my database?

Take your time and work out your answers before you start!

Once you have decided what you are storing, and what use you intend to make of the data, you are ready to start designing the database. Much of this can be done away from the computer.

## What fields do you need?

You must break the data down into the smallest units (fields) that you will want to store, search or sort on.

If you are setting up *names*, you would probably break the name into three fields – *Title*, *First name* (or *Initials*) and *Surname*. This way you can sort the file into Surname order, or search for someone using the First name and Surname.

If you are storing *addresses*, you would probably want separate fields for *Town/city*, *Region* and/or *Country*. You can then sort your records into order on any of these fields, or locate records by specifying appropriate search criteria. For example, using *Town/city* and *Country* fields, you could search for addresses in Washington (Town/city), USA (Country) rather than Washington (Town/city), UK (Country).

When planning your database, take a small sample of the data you wish to store and examine it carefully. This will help you confirm what fields will be required.

## Organize!

This is very important! Take note! **Organize** your data before you start. Decide **what** you want to store, and **what** you want to do with it. Work out what **fields** are required (for sorting and searching).

### How big are the fields?

You must also decide how much space is required for each field. The space you allocate must be long enough to accommodate the longest item that might go there. How long is the longest surname you want to store? If in doubt, take a sample of some typical names (Anderson, Johnston, Mackenzie, Harvey-Jones?) and add a few more characters to the longest one to be sure. An error in field size isn't as serious as an error in record structure as field sizes can be expanded without existing data being affected.

You can edit the structure of your table if necessary – but hunting through existing data to update records is time consuming, so it is best to get it right to start with!

It is *very important* that you spend time organizing and structuring your data *before* you start to computerize it – it will save you a lot of time and frustration in the long run!

# 1.8 Normalization of data

As well as deciding what you need to store, you also want to minimize any data duplication as far as possible. For example, in the library scenario you may want to keep a record of the name, address and contact details of the publishing company for each book you hold. You could keep this information in the same table as the book detail as illustrated below.

| Title | Author | Category | Library code | Number held | Publisher | Publisher address | Publisher telephone number |
|-------|--------|----------|--------------|-------------|-----------|-------------------|----------------------------|
|       |        |          |              |             |           |                   |                            |

We have already touched upon the fact that this approach could present some basic problems, the most obvious ones being:

- *Effort to maintain your data* – keeping the data up to date could result in a lot of work as the same publisher fields are in many book records. A change in the telephone number of a publisher would result in many fields having to be updated.

- *Size* – your database would end up much larger than necessary because all of the publisher detail would be repeated many times.

- *Accuracy* – having to key the same detail in several times can easily lead to errors.

The solution to this kind of problem is to use a process called *normalization*. As a result of normalization, you end up organizing your data fields into a group of tables, which can easily be linked when and as required.

The simple solution to the problem highlighted above is to create two tables – one for the book detail, and one for the publisher detail. In each table you would need a Publisher ID (or Publisher Code) field, that would be used to identify each publisher uniquely. This field could then be used to link the tables when and as required.

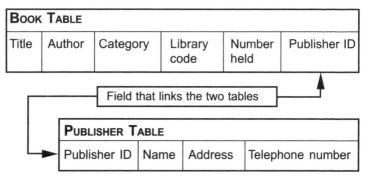

| Book Table | | | | | |
|---|---|---|---|---|---|
| Title | Author | Category | Library code | Number held | Publisher ID |

Field that links the two tables

| Publisher Table | | | |
|---|---|---|---|
| Publisher ID | Name | Address | Telephone number |

There are several benefits to this approach:

- Each set of publisher details is stored (and therefore keyed in) once only.

- The *Book* table will be considerably smaller in size than it otherwise would have been.

- Should any of the publisher details change (e.g. phone number) you only have one record to update (in the *Publisher* table).

* If you wrongly identify a publisher in a record in the *Book* table, you have one field only to correct, rather than all of the publisher's fields.

# 1.9 Starting Access

Starting from the Shortcut Bar:

1 Click the **Access** tool .

From the Start menu:

1 Click the **Start** button on the Taskbar.

2 Choose **Programs**.

3 Click **Microsoft Access**.

The Access window opens on your screen. You can use the Task Pane in this window.

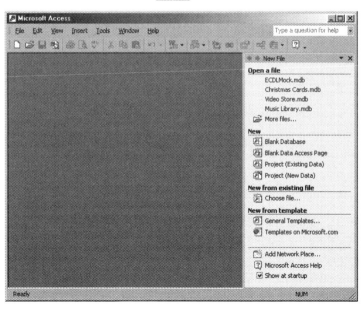

## Task Pane

When Access is installed on your machine, the Task Pane for creating and opening files is set to display at Startup. This means that the Task Pane appears down the right side of the screen each time that you start Access.

If you don't want the Task Pane displayed each time that you start Access, deselect the **Show at startup** checkbox at the bottom of the pane. The next time you start Access the Task Pane will not be displayed.

The New File Task Pane will appear automatically each time you click the **New** tool on the Standard toolbar.

**To create a new Access database or open an existing one:**

♦ Choose **Blank Database** and click **OK**.

You then arrive at the **File New Database** dialog box.

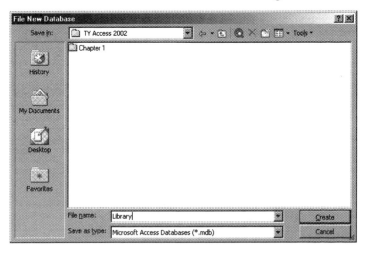

You must now decide where you want to store your database (My Documents is the default).

As with all Microsoft packages, a temporary filename is suggested for your database – in Access these follow the pattern db1, db2, db3 in each working session. You need to replace the temporary name with a name that means something to you, and reflects the contents of your database.

- If you are working through the project in this book, I suggest you call your database *Library* (as we are setting up a library database).

- Once you have named your database click the **Create** button.

This takes you through into Access, with your Library database window displayed.

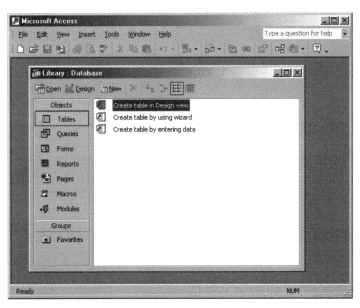

## 1.10 The Access screen

If you are familiar with other Windows packages, many of the items on the Access screen will appear familiar to you. A brief overview of the main areas follows, so we all know what's what!

You should be able to identify the following areas within the Access application window:

- Application Title Bar (where it says Microsoft Access)
- Application Minimize, Maximize/Restore and Close buttons (to the right of the Application Title Bar)

- Menu Bar (immediately under the Application Title Bar)
- Database toolbar (under the Menu Bar)
- Status Bar (at the bottom of the Application Window)
- Database Window.

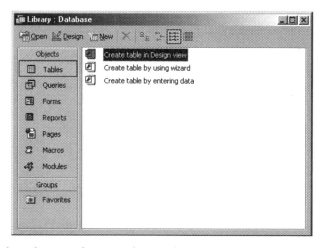

Within the *Database window* we have the:

- Database Title Bar
- Database Minimize, Maximize/Restore and Close buttons
- Database window toolbar
- Objects bar
- New object shortcuts
- Groups bar.

These areas will be referred to often during the course of this book, and in any other publications you read.

## Menus and toolbars

Office applications personalize your menus and toolbars automatically. The items that you use most often are featured on your personalized toolbars or menus.

Once you start using Access, you will find that the menu options most recently used will be displayed first when you open a menu (this is your personalized menu). You can expand the menus to reveal all commands (simply click on the down arrow that appears at the bottom of each menu). You may find that the menu automatically expands if you just wait once you have opened it. If you wish to modify the way that the menus work, open the **View** menu, choose **Toolbars**, **Customize**. You can switch on or off the *Always show full menus* or *Show full menus after a short delay* options on the **Options** tab.

*Don't panic if your toolbars and menus are not exactly the same as those illustrated in this book.*

# 1.11 Menus

There are seven main menus in the Access application window. You can use these menus to access any function or feature available. I suggest that you have a browse through them to get an idea of what is available – some menu items on the lists may appear familiar to you, some will be new.

You can display menus and select options using the mouse or the keyboard.

## Using the mouse

1  Click on the menu name to display the list of options available in that menu.

2  Click on the menu item you wish to use.

♦  Click the extension arrow at the bottom to display all the options available.

## Using the keyboard

Each menu name has one character underlined.

To open a menu:

♦  Hold down the [**Alt**] key and press the underlined letter, e.g. [**Alt**]-[F] for the **F**ile menu, [**Alt**]-[I] for the **I**nsert menu.

Each item in a menu list also has a letter underlined in it.

To select an item from the menu list either:

• Press the appropriate letter.

Or

• Use the up and down arrow keys on your keyboard until the item you want is selected, then press [**Enter**].

Once a menu list is displayed, you can press the right or left arrow keys to move from one menu to another.

To close a menu without selecting an item from the list:

• Click the menu name again, click anywhere off the menu list or press [**Esc**] on your keyboard.

In addition to the menus, many of the commands can be initiated using the toolbars, keyboard shortcuts or shortcut menus. Each of these areas will be covered as you progress through the book.

# 1.12  Help!

As you work with Access you will most probably find that you come a bit unstuck from time to time and need help! There are several ways of getting help – most of them very intuitive and user friendly.

### Ask a question box

You can access the Help system using the Ask a question box on the Menu Bar. Simply type in your question and press [**Enter**]. Choose the help topic required from the list that is displayed – click on it.

how do I create a table

● Define relationships between tables

● About creating a table

● Create a table from another table with a query

● Create a table

● About relationships in an Access database

▼ See more…

### Office Assistant

To call on the Office Assistant, press [**F1**] or click the **Microsoft Access Help** tool on the toolbar.

Depending on what you have been doing, the Assistant will display a list of topics that you might be interested in.

To choose a topic from the '*What would you like to do?*' list, simply click on the topic.

If you have a specific question you want to ask, type it in at the prompt and click the **Search** button.

The Help page will be displayed when you choose a topic from the list.

The Office Assistant can remain visible as you work on your file, or you can hide it and call on it as required. If you opt to leave it displayed, drag it to an area of your screen where it does not obscure your work.

- If you leave the Office Assistant displayed, left-click on it any time you want to ask a question.

- To hide the Office Assistant, right-click on it and choose **Hide** from the pop-up menu.

## To customize the Office Assistant

You can customize the Office Assistant to take on a different appearance, or behave in a different way.

1 Show the Office Assistant (press [**F1**] or click the **Microsoft Access Help** tool 🔲 ) if required, or click on the Assistant to display its Help window.

2 Click the **Options** button.

3 To change its appearance, select the **Gallery** tab and browse through the options available (use the **Next** and **Back** buttons to move through the various guises).

- If you find an Assistant you would like to use, click **OK**.

- To leave the Assistant as it was, click **Cancel**.

4 To change its behaviour, select the **Options** tab, select or deselect the options available as required – click on an

option to switch it on or off. A tick in a box means an option is selected, an empty box means it is not.

- If you do not want to use the Office Assistant, you can switch it off on the **Options** tab – simply deselect the *Use the Office Assistant* checkbox.

5 Click **OK** to set the options selected or **Cancel** to leave things as they were.

## Tips

Web Folders let you save and open your Office documents from a Web server. To add a Web Folder, click the Create New Folder button in the File Open dialog and provide a Web server URL.

OK

The Office Assistant is constantly monitoring your actions. If it thinks that it has a tip that may be useful to you, a bulb will light up beside it.

- To read its tip, click the bulb.

## The Help system

Whether or not you use the Office Assistant, the **Microsoft Access Help** tool 🔲 will open the on-line Help system. You can also access the Help system from the Help menu.

If you access the Help system through the Office Assistant, the Help page requested is displayed on the screen.

If you have switched the Office Assistant off, the Help tabs are also displayed when you access the Help system. You can interrogate the Help system using the Contents, Answer Wizard or Index tabs.

- Click the 🔲 tool to toggle the display of the tabs.

Some Help pages contain text in a different colour – usually blue. If the text is part of a list at the top of a Help page it indicates a link to a different area of the current Help page. If the coloured text is embedded within the main text on a page it is probably a phrase or some jargon that has an explanation or definition attached to it. Simply click the coloured text to display the definition.

Any sub-topics will be listed at the end of the Help page – to display a sub-topic simply click on it.

• When you have finished exploring the Help system, click the **Close** button ⊠ at the top right of the Help window.

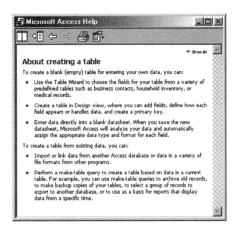

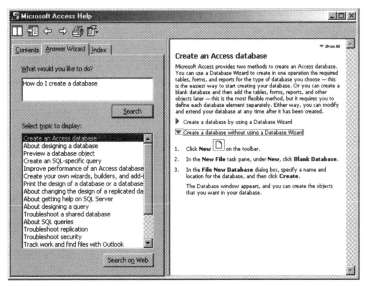

## Contents tab

You can 'browse' through the Help system from the Contents tab.

Click ⊞ to the left of a book to display or ⊟ to hide its list of contents.

When a book is open, you will see a list of topics.

**To display a topic:**

1 Click on it.

2 Work through the Help system until you find the help you need.

**To print a topic:**

• Click the **Print** tool 🖨 in the Help window when the topic is displayed.

**To revisit pages you have already been to:**

• Click the **Back** tool ⬅ or **Forward** tool ➡ to go back and forward through the pages.

Close the Help window when you have finished.

## Answer Wizard

If you want to interrogate the Help system by asking a question, try the Answer Wizard tab.

1 Enter a question, e.g. *How do I create a table,* and click **Search**.

2 Select a topic from the *Select topic to display* list.

• The Help page will be displayed.

## Index tab

If you know what you are looking for, the Index tab gives you quick access to any topic and is particularly useful once you are familiar with the terminology used in Access.

1 At the **Microsoft Access** dialog box, select the **Index** tab.

2 Type the word you are looking for in the *Type keywords* field and click **Search**.

Or

3 Double click on a word in the *Or choose keywords* list.

4 Choose a topic from the *Choose a topic* list.

5 Work through the Help system until you find what you are looking for.

6 Close the Help window when you have finished.

## What's This?

If you have not used Office before, or if you are new to Windows, there will be many tools, menus, buttons and areas on your screen that puzzle you. The *What's This?* feature can help you here – it works best when a database is open, as most of the tools, menus and screen areas are then active.

**To find out about an item in a menu list:**

1  Hold down the [**Shift**] key and press [**F1**].

2  Open the menu and select the option required.

**To find out about a tool or anything else in the application window:**

1  Hold down the [**Shift**] key and press [**F1**].

2  Click on the item.

If you accidentally invoke the *What's This* help option, press [**Shift**]-[**F1**] (or the [**Esc**] key) to cancel it.

## ScreenTips

If you point to any tool on a displayed toolbar, a ScreenTip will probably appear to describe the purpose of the tool. If no ScreenTips appear, you can switch them on if you want.

**To switch ScreenTips on or off:**

1  Point to any toolbar and click the right mouse button.

2  Choose **Customize...** from the shortcut menu.

3  In the **Customize** dialog box select the **Options** tab.

4  To switch ScreenTips on, select the *Show ScreenTips on*

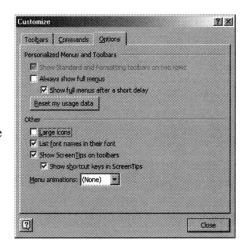

*toolbars* option (if you do not like ScreenTips, deselect this option to switch them off).

5 Click **Close**.

## Dialog Box Help

When you open a dialog box in Access, e.g. the Customize one below, you can get help on any item within it that you do not understand.

**To get help on an item in a dialog box:**

1 Click the **Help** button [?] at the right of the dialog box title bar.

2 Click on the option, button or item that you want explained.

+ A brief explanation of the item will be displayed.

> Increases the size of toolbar buttons so that they are easier to see.

3 Click anywhere in the dialog box to cancel the explanation.

# 1.13 Help on the Internet

If you cannot find the help you need in the normal Help system, visit the *Office on the Web* site for updated Help files, answers to top support issues and frequently asked questions on Access, tips and templates.

1 Open the **Help** menu.

2 Choose **Office on the Web**.

3 Navigate your way through the Help pages until you find the information required.

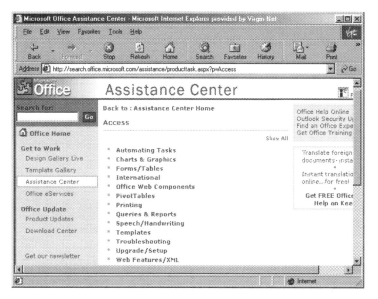

# 1.14 Closing your database

When working within Access you can close a database without closing the application itself.

**To close the database:**

* Click the **Close** button ⊠ on the Database window title bar.

# 1.15 Exiting Access

When you have finished working in Access you must close the application down – do no just switch off your computer!

**To exit Access:**

* Open the **File** menu and choose **Exit**.

Or

* Click the **Close** button ⊠ in the right-hand corner of the Application Title Bar.

# Summary

This chapter has introduced you to Access. We have discussed:

* What a database is and what it might be used for (there are many other examples throughout the book).

* Database jargon that might be new to you, but that will become part of your language as you use databases.

* Access Objects – the basic components of an Access database.

* System requirements and installation procedures (if you are buying a new computer and Access software you could get the package pre-installed).

* The importance of planning and organizing your data.

* The procedure known as *normalization*.

* Getting into Access using the Start menu and the Microsoft Office Shortcut Bar.

* The Access application window and the identification of the various areas therein.

* Utilizing the menu structure using the mouse and the keyboard.

* The on-line Help system and the various options available to help you to find the assistance you need.

* How to close Access down successfully when you have finished working with it.

# 02

## database design

**In this unit you will learn**

- how to start planning your database
- about data normalization
- about table relationships
- how to create a database
- how to open an existing database

## Aims of this chapter

This is where the real work begins! In this chapter you will learn how to design a database. We will discuss drawing up a task list and working out what fields we need, identify field types and discuss field properties. We will then consider how to minimize the duplication of data and discuss how the tables relate to each other within the database. Finally we will discuss how to create new and open existing database files.

# 2.1 The project

The main project in this book is the setting up of a Library database. The database will contain details of the books we have on our shelves, the authors, the publishers, and so on. We will limit the scope of the project to handling books, publishers and authors – library members' details and details of books borrowed will not be included at this stage.

Before you start working on the computer, there are three things you should do:

* Draw up a list of what is required from your database. Work out what you want to be able to do with your database. What tasks do you want to perform with it?

* Identify the fields required. Analyze the tasks and identify the data items (fields) you need to set up.

* Normalize your data to minimize redundant data – data that is duplicated unnecessarily can cause problems (see section 1.8).

# 2.2 Draw up a list of requirements

The first thing you must do is sit down and think! Before you start to do anything on the computer, work out what it is that you intend to do with your database. Make a list of all the things you want your database to be able to provide for you. What information do you want to record? What kind of questions will you want the system to provide answers to? What reports do you want to generate?

Using our Library database example, we might come up with the following list of things we would like to be able to do:

* Record, update and edit details of all the books held in the library – title, author, publisher, etc.
* Keep details of the different categories of book held, e.g. science, travel, cooking.
* Hold publisher details – name, address, telephone number, etc.
* Give the physical location of the book in the library – row, shelf number, etc.
* Provide details about the author of the book.
* Extract different sets of data, e.g.:
  * a list of all travel books from a specific publisher
  * a list of science and astronomy books by a given author.
* Prepare and print reports on various things:
  * details of books in specific categories
  * lists of books from a given publisher
  * lists of books by a particular author.

Once you have established what you want to be able to do with your database, you can start to plan how it might best be set up.

There are several things to consider here. In our example we want to record details of the books, publishers and authors of the books in our library. We want to be able to work with the data easily, without all the staff needing to become computer 'whizz kids' and we want to be able to extract selective details from our database and print out attractive reports! Sounds good!

# 2.3 Identify the detail required

You must now work out what detail you will need to store to enable your Access database to fulfil the requirements you have identified for it. Make a list of the tasks you want your database to perform.

Then consider each task individually, and write down what data items you think you will need for that task. A data item is simply a single piece of information about the thing you are working with – the book, author or publisher in our case. Include any notes that may be useful as you are working on your design. It is usually easy to think of the first few things you need, then it becomes harder as the list gets longer.

*Write down* the data items you come up with, and edit the list as you go through the process.

The use of a simple form can be handy here. Below are suggestions of what might be necessary for the list of requirements we have identified for the Library database.

**Task 1:** Record, update and edit details of all books held in the library – title, author, publisher, etc.

| Detail | Description | Notes |
|---|---|---|
| ISBN | Unique reference | Primary Key |
| Title | Book title | |
| Author | Personal details | Name, date of birth, date of death, nationality, specialist area, any other information |
| | | The information would be best held in a separate table, linked to the book table through the AuthorID. This approach would reduce unnecessary duplication of detail (which should mean a smaller database, with fewer errors). |
| Publisher | Contact details | Name, address, phone number, fax number, e-mail address |
| | | The information would be best held in a separate table, linked to the book table through the PublisherID. This approach would reduce unnecessary duplication of detail and help promote accuracy. |
| Category | e.g. Science, History, Music, Cookery | The categories could be held in a separate Categories table and detail would be 'looked up' from the book table |
| Location | Row and shelf number | |
| Copies | Number held | |
| Pub. Year | | |
| Price | | |
| Reference or Lending | Identifies reference or lending book | |

**Task 2:** Keep details of the different categories of book we hold, e.g. science, travel, cooking

| Detail | Description | Notes |
|---|---|---|
| Category name | Unique description of category | e.g. Science, History, Travel |

**Task 3:** Hold publisher details – name, address, telephone number, etc.

| Detail | Description | Notes |
|---|---|---|
| PublisherID | Unique identifier for each | Primary Key |
| Publisher Name | | |
| Publisher Address | | |
| Publisher Phone Number | | |
| Publisher Fax | | |
| Publisher e-mail address | | |

**Task 4:** Give the physical location of the book in the library – row, shelf number, etc.

| Detail | Description | Notes |
|---|---|---|
| Row Number ID | | |
| Shelf ID | | |

**Task 5:** Provide details about the author of the book

| Detail | Description | Notes |
|---|---|---|
| AuthorID | Unique identifier for each | Primary Key |
| Surname | | |
| Firstname | | |
| Date of Birth | | |
| Date of Death | | |
| Nationality | | |
| Speciality | | |
| Notes | | |

**Task 6:** Extract different sets of data from your database

♦ Ensure that table structure is broken down into the fields you want to sort and select on.

♦ Try to think of all the questions you might want to ask of your data, and set up the fields required when you specify the table structures. For example, if you want to be able to query your data to find out the titles of all the books you hold by a particular author, together with the publisher name and the year of publication, you will need to have a *Book Title* field, an *Author Name* field, a *Publisher* field and *Year Published* field somewhere in your database.

♦ Relational database structures are easy to edit, so it is possible to add, delete or edit fields that you make an error in at the set up stage. However, a bit of forward thinking at this stage can minimize the number of amendments that you will need to make in the future.

**Task 7:** Prepare and print reports on various things

♦ Ensure that table structure includes the fields required for the reports.

♦ Areas to consider here are as per the notes in the previous task.

♦ If you want to be able to produce a report grouping the books you hold under the heading *Publisher*, perhaps with an author grouping within the publisher grouping, the book titles sorted in ascending alphabetical order, and the total number of books held from each publisher displayed, you must have the fields required set up in the structure of your tables.

We also want to make the database easy to use. To facilitate this we could:

♦ Include validation checks on data to help reduce errors.

♦ Design a user friendly interface for staff.

Once you have completed this stage of the planning process, you can work out what fields will be required, how best to group the fields into tables and how the tables will be related to each other.

# 2.4 Normalization

When deciding on the tables required, you should consider how best to group the fields to minimize the duplication of data throughout the database – this is what is meant by the process of *normalization*.

## Table structure

Using the information contained in the lists above, we might decide to record all the Book details in one table, but use a separate table for the Publisher detail and a separate table for the Author detail. We could also have a fourth table that contains a list of the different categories of book. You must decide which fields should be in each table.

You must also decide what kind of data will be held in each field – will it be text, numbers, date, currency and so on.

### Primary Key

You should identify a field (or combination of fields) that would uniquely identify each record held within each table. This field (or group of fields) would be the *Primary Key* for the table. In our example a single field in each table would be sufficient for the Primary Key. In the *Book* table the *ISBN* would be different for each book, so this would make the ideal Primary Key for the *Book* table. Each Publisher would have their own ID, so this would be the field to choose for the Primary Key, and each Author would have their own ID, so the *AuthorID* would be the field to choose for the Primary Key in the *Author* table.

By breaking the detail down into four tables in this way, the details on each publisher would need to be recorded only once, in the *Publisher* table. The details on each author would also need to be recorded only once, in the *Author* table. The *Category* names would need to be entered only once. Within the *Book* table, you would simply need to enter the publisher, author and category codes in the appropriate fields and these would facilitate the link through to the other tables when required.

Details of the book's location within the library could be held in the main book table – there is no real benefit to be derived from placing this in a separate table.

## Book table

The field list for the *Book* table (together with possible data types) would therefore be:

| Book Table | | |
|---|---|---|
| **Field Name** | **Data Type** | **Notes** |
| ISBN | Text | Primary Key |
| Title | Text | |
| AuthorID | Number | |
| PublisherID | Number | |
| Name | Text | Look up Category Name field |
| Row Number | Number | |
| Shelf Number | Number | |
| Number Held | Number | |
| Publication Year | Number | Year only held |
| Price | Currency | |
| Reference or Lending | Text | |

## Publisher table

The field list for the *Publisher* table (with data types) would be:

| Publisher Table | | |
|---|---|---|
| **Field Name** | **Data Type** | **Notes** |
| PublisherID | AutoNumber | Primary Key |
| Publisher Name | Text | |
| Publisher Address | Text | |
| Publisher Phone Number | Text | |
| Publisher Fax | Text | |
| Publisher e-mail address | Text | |

## Author table

The field list for the *Author* table (with data types) would be, as shown overleaf:

| Author Table | | |
|---|---|---|
| **Field Name** | **Data Type** | **Notes** |
| AuthorID | AutoNumber | Primary Key |
| Surname | Text | |
| Firstname | Text | |
| Date of Birth | Date | |
| Date of Death | Date | |
| Nationality | Text | |
| Speciality | Text | |
| Notes | Text | |

## Category table

We can use another table to identify the category of book. By doing this, the full name of the book category would need to be keyed in only once, but it could be 'looked up' from the *Book* table at any time using a 'Look Up' option.

| Category Table | | |
|---|---|---|
| **Field Name** | **Data Type** | **Notes** |
| Category name | Text | Primary Key |

So, by using some forward planning, we have reached the stage where we have decided that a database consisting of four tables is just what we need for this situation.

# 2.5 Relationships

The *Book* table in our database is related to each of the other tables within the database as indicated below.

| Table | Related to | Joining Fields | Type of Relationship |
|---|---|---|---|
| Publisher | Book | PublisherID | One-to-many |
| Author | Book | AuthorID | One-to-many |
| Category | Book | Category Name | One-to-many |

The type of relationship in each case is one-to-many (this is the most common type of relationship between tables). One record in the *Publisher* table may be related to many records in the *Book* table – our library contains lots of books from each publisher. One record in the *Author* table may be related to many records in the *Book* table – many authors have written more than one book. One record in the *Category* table may be related to many records in the *Book* table – there are many books in each of our book categories. The tables are related to each other as shown in this diagram.

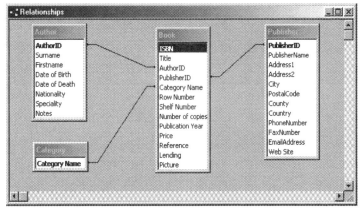

The lines between the tables indicate which fields are related to each other – these are called *join lines* in Access.

The Primary Key in each table is shown in bold – the relationships we need are between the Primary Key of the *Author, Publisher* and *Category* tables and the appropriate *foreign key (*the *Primary Key* viewed from another table) in the *Book* table.

You will learn how to define the table structures and set the relationships in Chapter 3.

## 2.6  Creating a new database

We are now ready to define the structures for our tables. If you have not created your library database file and do not have Access currently up and running, go into Access as described in Chapter 1 and create a database file called *Library*.

### Create a new database from within Access

If you have not yet created the *Library* database file:

1  Click the **New** tool 🗋 on the Database toolbar.

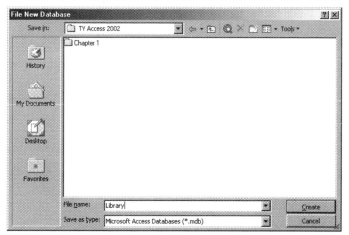

2  Choose **Blank Database** from the **New File** Task Pane.

3  Specify the folder you wish to save your database into.

4  Give the database a name.

5  Click **Create**.

If you have set up your *Library* database, but have closed it or exited Access, you must open the database again to work on it.

# 2.7 Opening an existing database

1  If Access is not already up and running, start it now.

2  On the New File Task Pane, select the *Library* database from the **Open a file** list.

3  Click **OK**.

♦  Your *Library* database will appear on your screen.

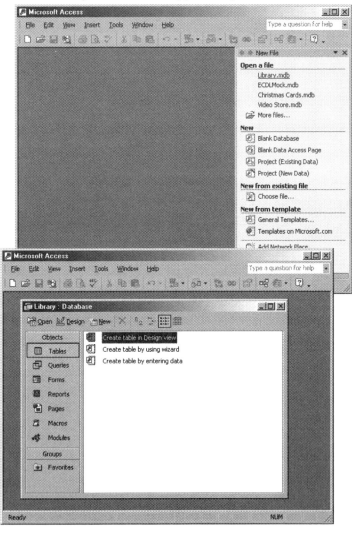

## Open an existing database from within Access

If Access is already running:

1 Click the **Open** tool 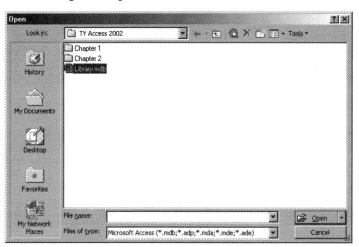 to display the **Open** dialog box.

2 Locate the folder that contains your database (probably *My Documents*, but you may have saved it somewhere else) and select the *Library* database from the file list displayed.

3 Click **Open** to open the database.

---

## Opening from the File menu

If the database you wish to open has been used recently, you may find it listed at the end of the **File** menu. To open a file from the recently used file list, open the menu, then click on the file name you require. The four most recently used files are listed at the end of the **File** menu.

---

Whether you have created a new database, or opened an existing one, the *Library Database* window should now be displayed on your screen.

# Summary

In this chapter we have tried to introduce you to the ground work required before you start to set up the tables in your Access database. We have discussed:

* Drawing up a list of requirements.

* Requirements analysis and field identification.

* Normalization of data.

* Relationships between tables.

* Creating a new database file.

* Opening an existing database file.

# 03

## table definition

**In this unit you will learn**

- how to define a table in Design view
- about the different data types and their properties
- how to set up a table using Table Wizard

## Aims of this chapter

Once you have worked out the database design it is time to
start setting up the table structures within your database.
In this chapter we will look at the options available when
defining the table structure – whether you do it manually, or
using a Wizard. We will then set up the relationships
between the tables we define.

# 3.1 Creating the table structure

1   Select **Tables** on the Objects bar within your **Database** win-
dow and click 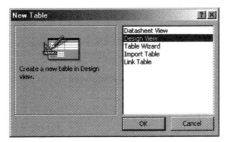.

2   At the **New Table** dialog box, select **Design View** and click
**OK**.

Or

*   Double click Create table in Design view in the database window
to display the design grid.

### Design view

Your new table is displayed in Design view on your screen. In
Design view you can specify the field names, data types and
any other properties you think would be useful.

The Design view window has two panes – an upper one where
you specify the field name, data type and description, and a
lower one where you specify the field properties. You can move
from one pane to the other by pressing the [**F6**] key on your
keyboard. The Table Design toolbar is displayed.

- To move from column to column in the upper pane, press the [Tab] key on your keyboard. You can also point and click with your mouse to move around the window.

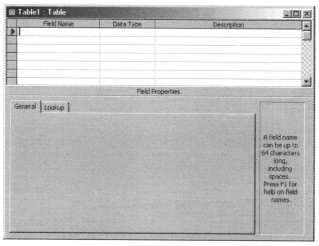

## 3.2 Data types and properties

### Data types

There are ten different data types to choose from when setting up your table structures. Brief notes on each type are given in the table below for your information. Most of your fields will probably be **Text**, with a few of the others used in each table depending on the type of data you wish to store.

| Data Type | Usage | Size | Notes |
|---|---|---|---|
| Text | Alphanumeric data | up to 255 bytes | Default data type |
| Memo | Alphanumeric data | up to 64 Kbytes | Cannot be indexed |
| Number | Numeric data | 1,2,4 or 8 bytes | |
| Date/Time | Dates and times | 8 bytes | Values for the years 100 through to 9999 |
| Currency | Monetary data | 8 bytes | Accurate to 4 decimal places and 15 digits to the left of the decimal separator |
| AutoNumber | Unique long integer created by Access for each new record | 4 bytes | Cannot be updated Useful for primary key fields |

| Yes/No | Boolean data | 1 bit | Yes and No values, and fields that contain 1 of 2 values On/Off, True/False |
|---|---|---|---|
| OLE Object | Pictures, graphs or OLE objects from other Windows applications | Up to 1 gigabyte | Cannot be indexed |
| Hyperlink | Inserts a 'hot spot' that lets you jump to another location on your computer, on your intranet or on the Internet | The address can contain up to 3 parts (each part can be up to 2048 characters) | The 3 parts are: Text to display* Address Subaddress* Screentip* * optional |
| Lookup | Lets you look up values in another table or from a combo box | The same as the Primary Key used to perform the look up | Choosing this option starts the Lookup Wizard to define the data type |

## Properties

You can customize each field by specifying different properties. These vary depending on the data type. The properties you will encounter are listed next:

| Property | Data Type | Notes |
|---|---|---|
| Field Size | Text and Number | Text from 1 – 255 characters |
| | Number field sizes are: ♦ Byte (single byte) ♦ Integer (2-byte) ♦ Long Integer (4-byte) ♦ Single (4-byte) ♦ Double (8-byte) | Values: ♦ 0 – 255 ♦ -32,768 to +32,767 ♦ -2,147,483,648 to 2,147,483,648 ♦ $-3.4 \times 10^{38}$ to $3.4 \times 10^{38}$ ♦ $-1.797 \times 10^{308}$ to $+1.797 \times 10^{308}$ |
| Format | | Options depend on the data type |
| Decimal places | Number and Currency | Auto (displays 2 d.p. for most formats except General Number, where decimal places depend on the precision of the number) or Fixed – 0 to 15 d.p. |
| Input Mask | Text, Number, Currency and Date/Time | Uses special characters to show the type of input allowed, and whether or not input is required See notes on input masks below |
| Caption | | For display on forms and reports |
| Default Value | All data types except Memo, OLE Object and AutoNumber | |

| Validation Rule | | You can supply an expression that must be true when you enter or edit data in this field |
|---|---|---|
| Validation Text | | You can specify the message to appear on the screen when a validation rule is not met |
| Required | | Set to Yes if data must be entered |
| Allow zero length | Text, Memo and Hyperlink fields | |
| Indexed | Text, Number, Currency, Date/Time and AutoNumber types | Indexing speeds up access to its data – fields that will be sorted or queried on should be indexed |
| Unicode Compression | Text, memo and Hyperlink fields | Worldwide character encoding standard. Leave at default - *Yes* |
| IME Mode | Text, memo, Date/time, | Leave at default settings |
| IME Sentence Mode | Hyperlink | |

## Input Mask character descriptions

| | |
|---|---|
| 0 | Digit (0-9), entry required. Plus (+) and Minus (-) signs not allowed |
| 9 | Digit or space. Plus (+) and Minus (-) signs not allowed |
| # | Digit or space, Plus (+) and Minus (-) signs allowed |
| L | Letter (A-Z), entry required |
| ? | Letter (A-Z) |
| A | Letter or digit, entry required |
| a | Letter or digit |
| & | Any character or space, entry required |
| C | Any character or space |
| < | Convert following characters to lower case |
| > | Convert following characters to upper case |
| ! | Causes input mask to fill from right to left when characters on the left side of the input mask are optional |
| \ | Causes the following character to be displayed as a literal character, i.e. \L is displayed as L. Entry required. |
| . , : ; - / | Decimal placeholder and thousand, date and time separators |

## Additional notes

* An input mask can contain up to three sections, separated by a semi-colon, e.g.

  99/99/00;0;_

◆ The first part specifies the pattern for the mask itself.

◆ The second part specifies whether or not any literal display characters are stored with the data. The default value is 0 meaning that they are; 1 means that only the data is stored.

◆ The final part sets the character used to display spaces in the input mask at data entry. The default is the underline character. If you want to use a space, enclose it in quotes, i.e.

99/99/00;0;" "

# 3.3 Defining the Category table

Using the field list tables we drew up earlier, we can set up the structure of our tables in Access. We will set up the *Category* table first. This **must** be set up before the *Book* table as the *Book* table will look up data from it. The records in the *Category* table have only one field containing the *Category name*.

Enter the name details in the first row of the upper pane.

1 In the **Field Name** column, key in the field name:

CategoryName

2 Press the [Tab] key to move along to the **Data Type** column and set this to **Text**.

◆ The default field size for a Text data type is 50 characters. This is more than is required for a category name, so this property could be reduced – 25 would be big enough.

3 Press [F6] to move to the lower pane (or click with the mouse) and change the field size from 50 to 25.

| Category table | | | |
|---|---|---|---|
| **Field Name** | **Data Type** | **Properties** | **Notes** |
| CategoryName | Text | Field Size = 25 | Primary Key |

### Establishing Primary Key status

Each category name will be different (unique) so we should give the field Primary Key status.

◆ To establish Primary Key status, click the **Primary Key** tool on the Table Design toolbar when the insertion point is anywhere in the *Category Name* field row in the upper pane.

Note that the **Index** property is automatically set to **YES** (**No Duplicates**) when a field is given Primary Key status.

### Save and close the table design

1   Click the **Save** tool  on the Design toolbar. If this is the first time you have saved the table the **Save As** dialog box will open.

2   Give your table a suitable name.

3   Click **OK**.

4   Click ⊠ to close the **Table Design** window.

Your new table will be listed under **Tables** in the **Database** window.

# 3.4 Defining the Book table

Once the *Category* table has been set up we can set up the *Book* table. Data types and the Properties for each field are suggested on the next page. Create a new table in Design View (see 3.1).

### Setting up the ISBN field

1   In the **Field Name** column, key in the field name – *ISBN* in our case.

2   Press the [**Tab**] key to move along to the **Data Type** column and set this to **Text**.

3   Press [**Tab**] to move along to the **Description** column and enter a field description if you wish.

### Field properties

1   Press [**F6**] to move to the lower pane (or click with the mouse) and change the field size from 50 to 20.

2   Set the **Required** property to *Yes* – a book must have an ISBN.

3   Press [**F6**] to return to the upper pane.

| Book table | | | |
|---|---|---|---|
| **Field Name** | **Data Type** | **Properties** | **Notes** |
| ISBN | Text | Field Size = 20<br>Required = Yes | Primary Key |
| Title | Text | Field Size = 50 | |
| AuthorID | Number | Long Integer | |
| PublisherID | Number | Long Integer | |
| Category Name | Text | Field Size = 25 | Value will be 'looked up' in the category table |
| Row Number | Number | Integer<br>Validation Rule<br>>=1 and <=40<br>Validation Text<br>'Enter a number between 1 and 40' | Rows numbered 1 – 40 if an incorrect entry is made, display the validation text message |
| Shelf Number | Number | Integer<br>Validation Rule<br>>=1 and <=6<br>Validation Text<br>'Enter a number between 1 and 6' | Shelves numbered 1–6, if an incorrect entry is made, display the validation text message |
| Number of copies | Number | Integer | |
| Publication Year | Number | Integer | As we are entering only the year use Number data type |
| Price | Currency | | |
| Reference | Yes/No | | |
| Lending | Yes/No | Default value = Yes | |
| Picture | OLE object | | Illustration for book |

## Establishing the Primary Key status

The *ISBN* field is the primary key for this table.

* Click the **Primary Key** tool 🔑 when the insertion point is anywhere in the *ISBN* field row in the upper pane.

Complete the structure for the rest of the table following the guidelines in the table opposite. See notes below regarding the *CategoryName* field specification.

Any field that you think you will want to sort on or query should be indexed. This enables Access to sort or select on that field faster than it would be able to do on a non-indexed field.

## CategoryName Field

1 Select **Lookup Wizard…** from the **Data Type** list. This invokes the wizard to walk you through the set up process.

2 At the first dialog box, choose 'I want the lookup column to look up the values in another table or query' and click **Next** (you want to look up the values in the *Category* table).

3 Select the *Category* table from the list and click **Next**.

4 Move the *CategoryName* field from the **Available Fields:** list to the **Selected Fields:** list (select the *CategoryName* field in the **Available Fields:** list and click the top button between the two lists to move it over) and click **Next**.

5 Adjust the width of the column if necessary (instructions are on the screen) and click **Next**.

6 Check the suggested column label, and change it if you wish – I suggest you change it to *Category*, as that is the data that will be displayed in the column.

7 Click **Finish**.

8 You will be prompted to save the table on completion of the Wizard. I suggest that you choose '*Yes*' (even if you have not set up the whole table structure yet) and name it *Book*.

The completed structure should be similar to this:

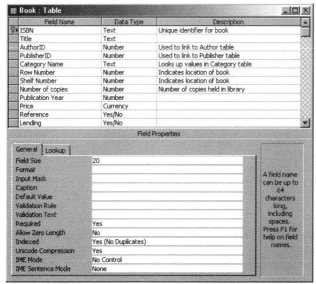

## Save the table design

♦ When you have finished setting up the whole table remember to **Save** 🖫 the *Book* table and **Close** ⊠ the **Table Design** window.

If you have already saved an earlier version of the table, clicking the *Save* tool will replace the old version of the table on your disk with the new one.

# 3.5  Defining the Author table

The Author table is set up in a similar way. Set up the design for the Author table following the guidelines below.

| Author table | | | |
|---|---|---|---|
| **Field Name** | **Data Type** | **Properties** | **Notes** |
| AuthorID | AutoNumber | Long Integer | Primary Key |
| Surname | Text | Size = 20<br>Indexed = Yes<br>Duplicates OK | |
| Firstname | Text | Size = 20<br>Indexed = Yes<br>Duplicates OK | |
| Date of Birth | Date/Time | Pick a Format<br>Input mask =<br>99/99/0000 | Type in the code, or click the<br>Build button beside the Input<br>Mask field and work through<br>the Wizard |
| Date of Death | Date/Time | Pick a Format<br>Input mask =<br>99/99/0000<br>the Wizard | Type in the code, or click the<br>Build button beside the Input<br>Mask field and work through |
| Nationality | Text | Size = 25<br>Indexed = Yes<br>Duplicates OK | |
| Speciality | Text | Size = 20<br>Indexed = Yes<br>Duplicates OK | Enter description:<br>'Main area of author's work' |
| Notes | | Memo | |

♦ **Save** 🖫 the *Author* table and close ⊠ the **Table Design** window.

# 3.6 Table Wizard

The last table structure to be set up is the *Publisher* table. This is essentially just a name and address table which could be set up manually, just as we have set up the other three tables. We could also consider using a Wizard to help automate the setting up of this table. Wizards can save you time when it comes to setting up a table structure – there are several provided with often-used structures for different situations, including name and address structures.

1 Select **Tables** on the Objects bar in the **Database** window and click **New**.

2 At the **New Table** dialog box, choose **Table Wizard**.

3 Click **OK**.

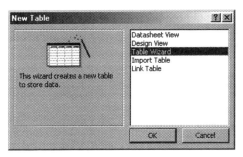

Or

4 Double click <kbd>Create table by using wizard</kbd> in the **Database** window to display the **Table Wizard** dialog box.

*At the Table Wizard dialog box:*

5 Select the **Business table** classification.

6 Choose **Suppliers** from the list of **Sample tables:** (the publishers are the suppliers for our library).

---

## See what the Wizard offers

At some stage, have a browse through the tables listed in both the Business and Personal classifications. You can save yourself a lot of time setting up a basic table structure by using a Wizard.

7  Select the fields required (one field at a time) from the **Sample Fields:** list and add them to the **Fields in my new table:** list (click the top button ⬛ between the two lists).

8  To add all the fields from the **Sample Fields:** list to the **Fields in my new table:** list, click the second button ⬛.

9  To remove a field from the **Fields in my new table:** list, select it and click the third button ⬛, or click the last ⬛ to remove all the fields from the  list.

Your list should be similar to the one shown below:

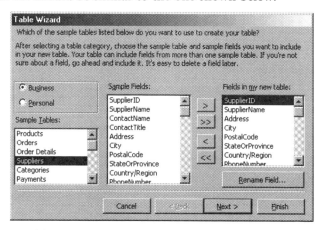

As our table is really going to contain details of the Publishers we use, we could change some of the field names to reflect this.

## Renaming a field

**To rename a field, e.g.** *SupplierID* **to** *PublisherID*:

1  Select *SupplierID* in the **Fields in my new table:** list.

2  Click the **Rename Field** button.

3  Enter a new name in the **Rename field** dialog box.

4  Click **OK**.

Do this for any other fields you wish to rename – *SupplierName* could become *PublisherName*, *StateOrProvince* could become *County*.

5   When you are satisfied with the field names, click the **Next** button to move on to the next step in the Wizard.

6   The Wizard automatically suggests a name for your table – edit the table name if necessary – *Publisher* table would perhaps be a more suitable name than *Suppliers* in this case.

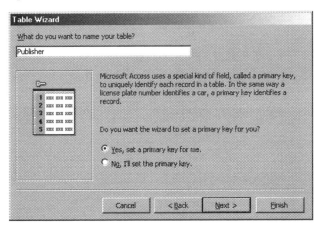

7   At the **Primary Key** options, let Access set the Primary Key – the *PublisherID* field will be made the Primary Key.

8   Click **Next** to move on to the next step.

## Checking relationships

The dialog box displays the relationships between your new table and any tables you have already set up in your database. Sometimes Access relates the tables automatically using the field names and properties, other times it fails to make a relationship and you must tell it what relationships exist.

The *Publisher* table should be related to the *Book* table in a one-to-many relationship – one record in the *Publisher* table may have many related records in the *Book* table as we may have several books from the same publisher.

If Access has not made the relationship, or if you wish to check that Access has made the correct relationship between your tables:

1 Select the row that specifies the relationship status to the *Book* table.

2 Click the **Relationships...** button.

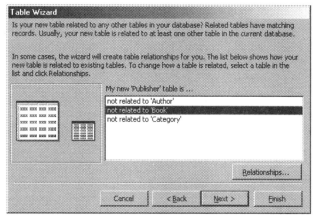

3 At the **Relationships** dialog box, check the relationship status. The second one should be selected – one record in the *Publisher* table may be related to many in the *Book* table.

4 Select this option if necessary.

5 Click **OK**.

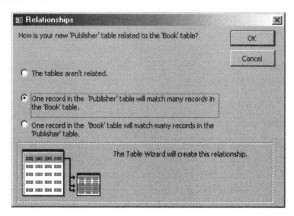

6 Click **Next** to move on to the final step in the Wizard.

When you reach the checkered flag, you know you have reached the final step in your Wizard.

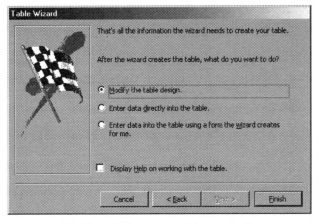

7   Select **Modify the Table Design** (this will allow us to check that the field properties are set up the way we want them).

8   Click **Finish**.

You will be taken through to the **Design** window for the *Publisher* table you have just set up.

◆   Move through the fields, checking the properties in the lower pane as you go.

---

## The masked danger!

Beware of input masks set up for postcode, phone and fax numbers. These will follow US conventions and will cause problems when we enter data using UK or European layouts.

---

### Deleting input masks

Delete any input masks from the lower pane for these fields.

1   Click anywhere in the appropriate field row in the upper pane.

2   Move to the lower pane (press [**F6**]).

3   Select the **Input Mask** detail (click and drag over it).

4   Press the [**Delete**] key on your keyboard.

You may also notice detail in the **Caption** property for some fields – the phone, fax and e-mail fields for example. Anything keyed into the Caption property will appear as a label on any Form using that field – see Chapter 6 on Forms Design.

5  **Save** 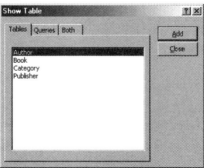 the changes you have made to the design of the *Publisher* table and **Close** ☒ the table.

---

## Hyperlink field

Most publishers will have a Web site where you can find out about them and the books that they have to sell. It may be useful to have a hyperlink field in the Publisher table so that you can easily visit these Web sites. You should add a new field to the end of the field list in the Publisher table to facilitate this – Field Name: Web Site, Data Type: Hyperlink.

---

You will be returned to your **Database** window, where all four tables are listed on the **Tables** tab.

# 3.7 Relationships

Before moving on you should check the relationships between the tables in your database and modify any that are not correct.

* To check the relationships between your tables, click the **Relationships** 🔲 tool on the Database toolbar.

If relationships have been created between tables during table definition, the **Relationships** window opens. This displays the tables in your database and any existing relationships.

* If no relationships have been set up, the Show Table dialog box appears.

If all the tables are not displayed, you can easily add them to the **Relationships** window.

1  Click the **Show Table** 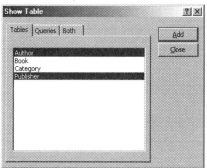 tool to display a list of the tables in your database.

2  Select the table (or tables) you wish to add to the **Relationships** window and click the **Add** button.

You can add several tables to the **Relationships** window at the same time if you wish.

If the tables are listed next to each other in the **Show Table** dialog box, select the first, then point to the last, hold down [**Shift**] and click – all the tables in the range will be selected.

If the tables are not next to each other, click on the first, then hold down [**Ctrl**] while you click on each of the other tables.

3  Click the **Close** button once you have added your tables.

Your **Relationships** window will contain all the tables and any relationships will be displayed.

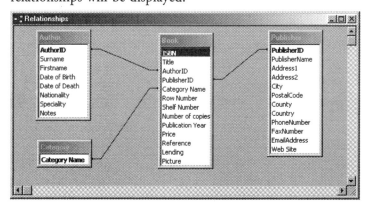

The lines running between the tables are called *join lines*. The join lines run between the fields linking the tables. Access will often create the link between tables automatically, e.g. when you use the Lookup Wizard or create tables using the wizard.

• To remove a table or query from the relationship window, click on it, then press [**Delete**].

## Deleting and creating join lines

You can delete join lines and create other join lines as required.

**To delete an existing relationship:**

1 Click on the join line you wish to remove to select it.

2 Press the [**Delete**] key on your keyboard.

3 Respond to the prompt as required.

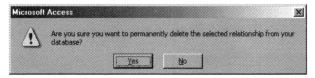

**To create a relationship:**

4 Click on the field you wish to relate to another table to select it.

5 Drag the selected field and drop it onto the field you wish to link it to in the other table.

6 If you want to check the type of relationship that will be created, click **Join Type...** to view the options in the **Join Properties** dialog box.

7 Change the type if necessary – all our join types should be option 1.

8 Click **OK**.

9 At the **Edit Relationships** dialog box, click **Create** to establish the relationship.

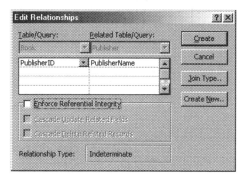

## Editing relationships

You can easily edit existing relationships.

1 Double-click the join line that you wish to edit.

2 Modify the settings in the **Edit Relationships** dialog box as necessary.

3 Click **OK**.

### Relationship type

**One-to-many** – one of the related fields is a primary key or contains a unique index. This is the most common type of relationship. In our example a record in the *Publisher* table can have many matching records in *Book*, but a record in the *Book* table has only one matching record in *Publisher* – a one-to-many relationship.

**One-to-one** – both the related fields are primary keys or contain unique indexes. Each record in the first table can have only one matching record in the second, and vice versa. One-to-one relationships are sometimes used to divide a table that has many fields, or to isolate some fields for security reasons. This type of relationship is not very common.

**Indeterminate** – neither of the related fields are primary keys or contain unique indexes.

## Referential integrity

These are the rules that are followed to preserve the defined relationships between tables when you enter or delete records.

If you enforce referential integrity, Access prevents you from:

* Adding records to a related table when there is no associated record in the primary table.

* Changing values in the primary table that would result in orphan (unconnected) records in a related table.

* Deleting records from the primary table when there are matching related records in a related table.

## Closing the Relationships window

Click 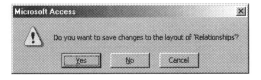 to save any changes you have made to the **Relationships** window. Close the **Relationships** window when you have finished.

If you close the **Relationships** window without saving your changes, you will be prompted to do so. Respond to the prompt as necessary.

You will be returned to the **Database** window.

---

## Summary

In this chapter we have discussed the alternative ways of defining the tables within your database:

* Defining a table in Design view.

* Data types available.

* Data properties.

* Defining a table using a Table Wizard.

* Checking, creating and deleting relationships between tables.

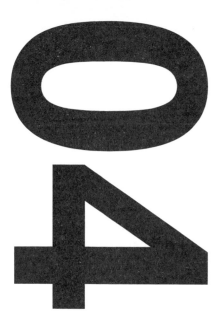

# 04

## data entry and edit

**In this unit you will learn**

- how to enter and edit data in the datasheet
- some formatting options for the datasheet
- how to move between the different table views
- how to create an autoForm

## Aims of this chapter

In this chapter we will start to enter data into our tables. Working in Datasheet view, we will look at the various options for data entry and edit together with display options for the datasheet. As an alternative to Datasheet view, we will use a simple form for data entry and edit.

# 4.1 Data entry in Datasheet view

If you are working through the project in this book, you should be in Access with your *Library* database open. The four tables that we defined in the previous chapter will be listed under **Tables** in the **Database** window.

You **must** enter data into the *Category* table before you can complete the *Book* table as the *Book* table will 'look up' data in the Category table.

I suggest you do the *Publisher*, *Author* and *Category* tables before the *Book* table – this way you will have the necessary codes for the *PublisherID*, *AuthorID* and *CategoryName* fields in the *Book* table. Data entry is very easy for the most part. You simply open the table and key in the data – using the [**Tab**] key or the mouse to move from field to field. As you are keying in the data, look out for the features mentioned below.

* To open a table in **Datasheet** view, double-click on the name, or select the table on the **Tables** tab and click **Open**.

In Datasheet view, a table looks similar to a spreadsheet layout – each record is presented in a row and each field in a column.

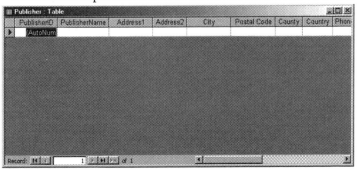

- To move forward through the fields press the [**Tab**] key.
- To move backwards through the fields press [**Shift**]–[**Tab**].
- Or click in the field you want to move to using the mouse.

> ## Project data
>
> If you are working through the library project in this book, key in the data suggested for all four tables. You will find suggested data for each of the tables in the Appendix.

## Publisher table

### AutoNumber

The *PublisherID* field has the AutoNumber data type – this field will be completed automatically by Access; you cannot enter any data into it.

- Press the [**Tab**] key to move from column to column, entering your publisher data.

When you complete a record (when you reach the last column):

- Press [**Tab**] to move on to the first column of the next record.

You may notice, as you key in your data, that the record you are currently writing to has a pencil icon in the row selector area to the left of the record.

| PublisherID | PublisherName | Address1 | Address2 | City | |
|---|---|---|---|---|---|
| 1 | Hodder & Stoughton Ltd | 338 Euston Road | | LONDON | N |
| 2 | Borthwick-Henderson | Applewood House | Applewood Hill | OXFORD | C |
| 3 | Westward Lock Ltd | 18 Clifftop Street | | LONDON | S |
| 4 | Softcell Press | One Softcell Rise | | ORLANDO | 3 |
| 5 | Christy Corporation | 20 E 103rd Street | | INDIANAPOLIS | 4 |
| 6 | Arrows Publications | Randall House | 1 Cavalier Bridge Road | LONDON | S |
| 7 | Harry Cousin Ltd | 10-23 Frosty Road | South Bank | LONDON | N |
| 8 | Beaver Books Ltd | 7 Squirrel Lane | | LONDON | W |
| 9 | Darling Kinghorn Ltd | 2 Herbert Street | | LONDON | N |
| 10 | City Publications Ltd | 7 Queen Street | | EDINBURGH | E |
| 11 | Scrambler Publication Ltd | 609 Prince Street | | LONDON | N |
| 12 | BPU Publications | Europa House | Queen's Cross | OXFORD | C |
| 13 | Outreach College Press | Wilson Way West | | LIVERPOOL | L |
| 14 | Carling & Sons plc | 4 St Thomas' park | | LONDON | S |
| 15 | Trueform Press plc | Manderson House | 8 George Street | EDINBURGH | E |

Record: 1 of 15

## Hyperlink

You should enter the URL (Uniform Resource Locator) of the Web site for each publisher in the Web Site field.

1 Click the **Insert Hyperlink** tool 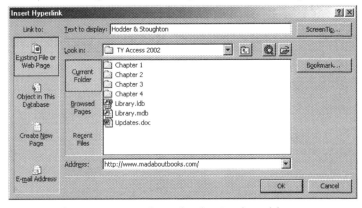 on the Table Datasheet toolbar.

2 Select *Existing File or Web Page* in the **Link to:** options.

3 Enter the text you wish to display in the table.
4 Type in the URL of the page you want to jump to.
5 Click **OK** at the **Insert Hyperlink** dialog box – your hyperlink text will be displayed, e.g. 'Hodder & Stoughton'.

To jump to a hyperlink location from your table, click on the hyperlink.

## Author table

### Input mask

When entering data to the *Author* table, note the effect of the input mask on the *Date of Birth* and *Date of Death* fields. When you enter data into these fields, the pattern set for the data appears and you just key in the figures.

Access also carries out its own validation tests on data that you key into a date field. If you try entering a date like 30/02/60 you will get an error message to indicate the date is not recognized.

| | AuthorID | Surname | Firstname | Date of Birth | Date of Death | Nationality | Speciality |
|---|---|---|---|---|---|---|---|
| + | 10 | Camember | Marion | | | French | Gardening |
| + | 11 | Meunier | Luc | | | French | Cooking |
| + | 12 | Allan | Isabelle | 10/05/1965 | | Scottish | Travel |
| + | 13 | Stephen | Moira | | | Scottish | Computing |
| + | 14 | MacDonald | Donald | 12/12/2020 | 01/03/1978 | Scottish | Travel |
| + | 15 | Williams | Peter | 10/10/1930 | | Irish | Science |
| + | 16 | Borthwick | Anne | | | Welsh | Astronomy |
| + | 17 | Ferguson | Alan | 04/12/1945 | | English | Computing |
| + | 18 | Wilson | Peter | 12/01/1930 | | Canadian | Children's Fic |
| + | 19 | Smith | Ann | | | American | Computing |
| + | 20 | Watson | George | 22/10/1945 | | Austrian | Travel |
| * | toNumber) | | | | | | |

Record: 20 of 20

## Description

If you look at the status bar when entering data into a field for which you keyed in a description during table definition, you will notice that the description text appears in the status bar when you are in that field, e.g. the *Speciality* field for the *Author* table.

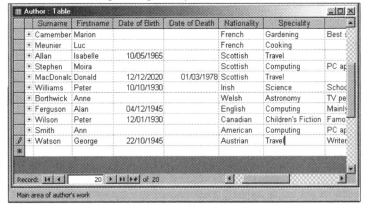

## Book table

### Category field

When the insertion point is in the *Category* field:

1 Click the **drop down arrow**.
2 Select the name required from the list (the entries in the list have been looked up in the *Category* table).

## Validation rules and validation text

Check out your validation codes in the *Row Number* and *Shelf Number* fields by entering a shelf number over 40 and a row number over 6.

## Yes/No fields

In the *Book* table we defined the **Yes/No** data type for the *Reference* and *Lending* fields. On entering data in Datasheet view notice that they are displayed as checkboxes.

* To register a 'Yes' there must be a tick in the box.
* To register a 'No' leave the box empty.

You can toggle the status of this field by clicking on the box.

## Default Value

Notice that the *Lending* field has been selected automatically for each record. This is because we set the Default Value to **Yes** when we defined the table.

## OLE Object

In the *Book* table we defined an OLE Object data type for the *Picture* field to allow us to insert a picture that reflected the book's subject.

**To insert an object into an OLE Object field in Datasheet view:**

1  Choose **Object...** from the **Insert** menu.

2  At the **Insert Object** dialog box select the object type required – in this example **Microsoft Clip Gallery**.

3  Click **OK**.

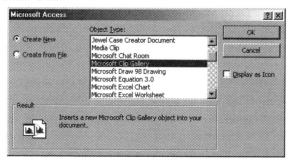

4  Select a picture to use in your OLE field and click **OK**.

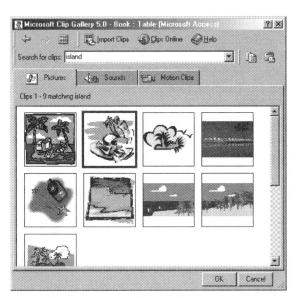

In Datasheet view the picture is not displayed, but the name of its original application – Microsoft Clip Gallery – is.

## 4.2 Datasheet and Design view

If you discover a problem with your table design, you can move from Datasheet view to Design view to fix it.

• To move from Datasheet view to Design view, click the **View** tool ![tool] on the Table Datasheet toolbar.

If you make any changes to the design of your table, you must save them. Be careful not to make any changes that will result in losing data that you need, e.g. making a field too small.

• To move back into Datasheet view, click the **View** tool ![tool] on the Table Design toolbar.

## 4.3 Editing in Datasheet view

### Moving through your table

We have already discussed the fact that you can move within and between records using the [**Tab**], [**Shift**]-[**Tab**] keyboard techniques, or by pointing and clicking in the desired field using the mouse.

At the bottom left of the table window the navigation buttons are displayed. These buttons can be used to help you move through your table in Datasheet view.

- The record number field tells you which record the insertion point is currently in, and to the right of this you will find the total number of records in your table.

- The Next ▶ and Previous ◀ Record buttons allow you to move forwards and backwards through your records, one at a time.

- The current field remains constant as you move up or down through your records – although you are moving from one record to another, the same field in each record is selected.

- The Last ▶▶ and First ◀◀ Record buttons move you through to the last or first record respectively.

- To go to a specific record number, select the record number in the record number field, enter the record number you wish to go to and press [**Enter**].

## Editing the field contents

If you spot an error in Datasheet view, you must position the insertion point within the field you wish to edit, and make whatever changes are required.

You can use the scroll bars (horizontal and vertical), or the navigation buttons to locate the record you need to update. Once the record has been located, the simplest technique is to click within the field that needs to be changed and insert or delete data as necessary.

If you use the [**Tab**] or [**Shift**]-[**Tab**] keyboard techniques to move through fields that contain data, the contents of a field are selected when you move on to it.

- To replace the selected data within a field, simply key in the new text – whatever you type will replace the original data.

- To delete the data in the field press the [**Delete**] key when the old data is still selected.

• To add or delete data *without* removing the current contents of the field, you must deselect the field contents before you edit.

To deselect the field contents, either click within the field using your mouse, or press the [F2] key on your keyboard. Once the data is deselected you can position the insertion point and insert or delete as required.

## Adding new records

Regardless of which record your insertion point is currently in, the **New Record** ▦ button or tool takes you to the first empty row at the end of your table to allow you to add a new record.

# 4.4  Formatting in Datasheet view

When working in Datasheet view, there are a number of formatting options you might like to experiment with.

Formatting the datasheet affects the whole table, not just the row or column the insertion point is in.

**To change the font:**

1  Choose **Font...** from the **Format** menu.

2  Complete the dialog box with details of the font style, size and attributes required.

3  Click **OK**.

**To change the datasheet format:**

1  Choose **Datasheet...** from the **Format** menu.

2  Specify the cell effect required, which gridlines you wish to show, the background colour, the gridline colour and the border and line styles.

3  Click **OK**.

**To change row height:**

1  Choose **Row Height...** from the **Format** menu.

2  Specify a row height, or select the **Standard Height** checkbox.

3  Click **OK**.

You can also use your mouse to change the row height.

1 Move the mouse pointer over the row selector area (the grey column to the left of the fields).

2 Position the mouse pointer over the dark line between two rows – you should get a black double-headed mouse pointer.

3 Click and drag up or down until the required height is reached.

**To change column width**:

1 To change the column width of a particular column, place the insertion point anywhere within the column.

2 Choose **Column Width...** from the **Format** menu.

3 Specify the width required or select **Standard Width**.

4 Click **OK**.

Alternatively, you can let Access work out the best size for the column by choosing **Best Fit**.

You can also resize the column width using the mouse.

1 Position the mouse pointer over the dark line to the right of the field name of the column you wish to change the width of – you should get a black double-headed mouse pointer.

2 Click and drag right or left to make the column to the left bigger or smaller.

To get Access to do a **Best Fit** sizing, double click the dark line to the right of the field name in the column you wish to resize.

# 4.5 Data entry in Form view

As an alternative to entering data into a table in Datasheet view, you could use Form view.

In Datasheet view, each record is displayed in a row, each field in a column. As many fields and records are displayed in the table window as will fit.

In Form view, the fields are arranged attractively on the screen (you can design forms to resemble paper forms you actually use) and one record is displayed at a time. Form view is often considered more user friendly than Datasheet view.

# AutoForm

AutoForm is a tool that builds a simple form automatically. You do not need any form design skills to use this. We will look at designing custom forms in Chapter 6.

## AutoForm from the Database window

To create an AutoForm for a table:

1 Select the table you wish to use from the **Tables** list in the **Database** window.

2 On the Database toolbar, click the drop-down arrow to the right of the **New Object** tool.

3 Choose **AutoForm**.

The table you selected is displayed using a simple form layout. The form shown here contains a subform with a list of books by each author. Subforms will be discussed in Chapter 6.

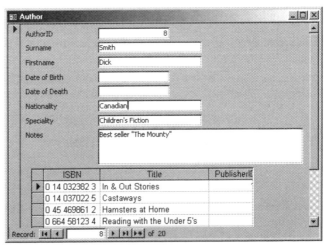

You can move around in Form view in the same way as you did in Datasheet view:

• Press [**Tab**] or [**Shift**]-[**Tab**] to move from field to field, or click in the field you want to input or edit.

* Use the navigation buttons to move from record to record, or to the first or last record in the table.

* To go to a specific record number, select the record number in the record number field, enter the record number you wish to go to and press [**Enter**].

* Click the **New Record** button to get a blank form on which to enter new data.

* If necessary, use the scroll bars to display parts of the form that are not displayed in the window.

The data you enter or edit in your form in Form view will be stored in the table on which the form is based. Even if you opt not to save the form itself, the data will still be stored.

Any fields defined as an OLE Object (e.g. the *Picture* field in the *Book* table) will display the object in Form view, but the name of the source application is shown in Datasheet view.

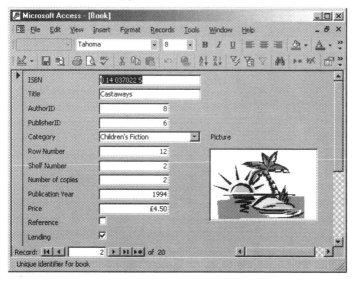

## AutoForm from Datasheet view

If you have been working on your table in Datasheet view, you can easily change to Form view using the New Object tool.

In Datasheet view, there is also a **New Object** tool on the Table Datasheet toolbar. Choose **AutoForm** from the drop-down list to display your datasheet in Form view.

## Changing views

When working with a form, you have three views of your table you can choose from – Design, Datasheet and Form.

**To change views:**

1 Click the **drop-down arrow** to the right of the **View** tool.

2 Click on the view required.

◆ Ignore the Pivot table for the time being.

## Saving your Form

**If you want to save your form:**

1 Click the **Save** tool on the Form view toolbar.

2 At the **Save As** dialog box, either accept the default form name, or edit it as required.

3 Click **OK**.

If you close your form without first saving it, Access will ask you if you want to save the form.

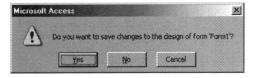

If you choose **Yes**, you will be taken to the **Save As** dialog box as described above. If you choose **No**, the form will close without being saved. If you click **Cancel**, you will be returned to Form view.

If you save your form, it will be listed under **Forms** in the **Database** window. You can open the form again at any time – either double click on the form name or select the form name and click **Open**.

# Summary

In this chapter we have considered the main options for entering and editing data in your tables. You have found out about:

+ Opening your tables in Datasheet view.

+ Entering and editing data in Datasheet view.

+ Moving between records.

+ Adding new records.

+ Formatting the datasheet.

+ Moving between the different table view options.

+ Creating a simple form using AutoForm.

+ Saving the Form.

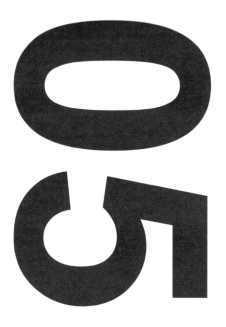

# 05 table manipulation

**In this unit you will learn**

- how to edit a table structure
- how to add and delete records
- about hiding and freezing columns
- how to preview and print your table

## Aims of this chapter

In this chapter you will learn how to manipulate the structure of your table – add fields, delete fields, change field properties and move fields. You will also learn how to add and delete records in Datasheet view, hide and unhide columns, freeze and unfreeze columns and print from Datasheet view.

# 5.1 Changing the table structure

To edit the table structure you must take the table into Design view. You can do this from the **Database** window if you select the table you need to edit on the **Tables** list, and click **Design**.

Alternatively, if you are already in Datasheet view, you can go into Design view by clicking the **View** tool 🔲.

### Adding a new field

♦ If the new field is to go at the end of the structure, scroll through the rows until you reach the empty row under the existing fields. Enter the field name, data type and properties as required.

**To add a new field between two existing fields:**

1 Place the insertion point in the upper pane anywhere within the field that will be below your new field.

2 Click the **Insert Rows** tool 🔲 on the Table Design toolbar – a new empty row is inserted above the current one.

3 Enter the field name, data type, etc. as required.

### Deleting a field

1 Place the insertion point in the upper pane within the field to be deleted.

2 Click the **Delete Rows** tool 🔲 on the Table Design toolbar.

3   Respond to the prompt – choose **Yes** to delete the field, **No** if you have changed your mind.

## Delete with care

Be careful when you delete fields – any data held in that field in your records will be lost.

### Changing the field properties

1   Place the insertion point in the upper pane within the field whose properties you are going to edit.

2   Press [**F6**] to move to the lower pane.

3   Edit the properties as required.

4   Press [**F6**] to return to the upper pane.

When changing a field size, watch that you don't end up losing data. If you reduce the field size, any record that has data in that field in excess of the new field size will have the extra characters chopped off!

### Primary Key

To change the field that has Primary Key status:

♦   In the upper pane, place the insertion point in the field that you want to take Primary Key status. Click the **Primary Key** tool 🔑.

To remove Primary Key status, and *not* give it to any other field:

♦   In the upper pane, place the insertion point in the field that has Primary Key status and click the **Primary Key** tool 🔑.

### Renaming a field

You can rename a field in either Design or in Datasheet view.

**To rename a field in Design view:**

◆ Edit the name in the first column in the upper pane.

**To rename a field in Datasheet view:**

1 Double click on the field name you want to change in the **Field Name** row.

2 Edit the field name as required.

3 Press [**Enter**] or click in the record detail area.

## 5.2 Rearranging the fields

You can move the fields in either Design view or Datasheet view.

### Design View

1 In the upper pane, click in the row selector bar to the left of the field you wish to move.

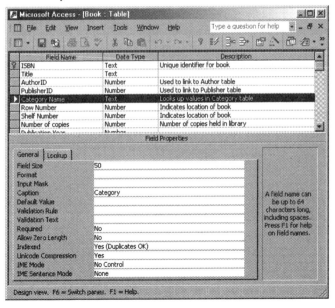

2 With the mouse pointer over the selector bar area, drag and drop the field into its new position – you will notice a thick dark horizontal line that indicates the position that the field will move to.

To keep the fields in their new position you must save the design before you close your table.

## Datasheet view

1 Select the field by clicking in the **Field Name** row above the field you wish to move.

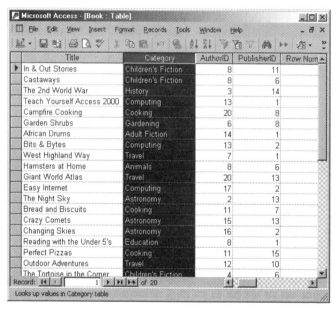

2 With the mouse pointer in the **Field Name** row, drag and drop the field into its new position – you will notice a thick dark vertical line indicating the position that the field will move to.

When you close your table, you will be asked if you wish to save the layout changes to your table.

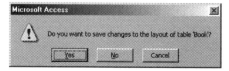

Choose **Yes** to save the changes, **No** to close the table without saving the changes, or **Cancel** to return to the table to do some more work.

# 5.3 Editing the datasheet

## Adding new records

When adding new records you add them to the end of the list of existing records:

1 Click the **New Record** tool 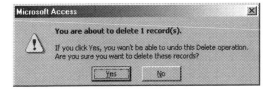 to move through to the first empty row under the existing records.

2 Key in your data.

## Deleting records

1 Place the insertion point within the record you wish to delete.

2 Click the **Delete Record** tool  on the Table Datasheet toolbar.

3 Respond to the delete prompt as required – choose **Yes** to confirm the deletion; choose **No** if you have changed your mind.

# 5.4 Subdatasheet

A subdatasheet is simply a datasheet that is nested within another datasheet. The subdatasheet will contain records that are related or joined to records in the first datasheet.

Access automatically creates a subdatasheet in a table that is in a one-to-one relationship, or is on the 'one' side of a one-to-many relationship, when the Subdatasheet Name property of the table is set to **Auto**. (You can check this setting from Design view for any table – click the Properties tool  on the

Table Design toolbar.) A relationship is defined by matching primary and foreign key fields in the related tables.

All of the tables in our database are related to at least one other in the database. The *Publisher*, *Author* and *Category* tables are each related to one table, *Book*, in a one-to-many relationship.

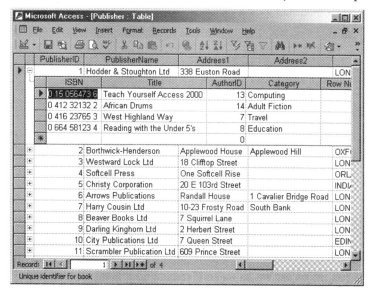

When looking at a table in Datasheet view, you can tell that it has a subdatasheet attached to it if the first column in the table is filled with ⊞ .

To view the related data, click the ⊞ to expand the subdatasheet.

To collapse the subdatasheet again, click ⊟ in the first column.

There may be times when you want to expand (or collapse) the subdatasheets of all records in the table displayed.

1 Open the **Format** menu.

2 Select **Subdatasheet**.

3 Choose **Expand All** or **Collapse All** as required.

You can enter and edit data in the main table or the subdatasheet as necessary.

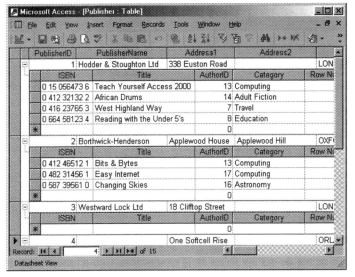

**To remove a subdatasheet link:**

1 Open the **Format** menu, select **Subdatasheet** then choose **Remove**.

• The left most column in your table will disappear and the link between the tables is gone.

**To restore the link again:**

1 Choose **Subdatasheet** from the **Insert** menu.

2 In the dialog box, select the table you want to link to, check/ edit the fields through which the tables are linked and click **OK**.

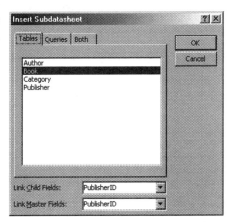

# 5.5 Hiding columns

When working in Datasheet view, the number of fields displayed and the horizontal scroll required to move from the first field to the last field in a record can make it difficult to view the data you require. You may find yourself scrolling back and forward checking and double checking field contents.

If you aren't interested in the contents of some fields for the time being, you can hide the fields you don't need.

*When you hide columns, they aren't deleted but simply hidden from view.*

To hide a field (or fields) you must first select the field(s).

**To select a single field:**

♦ Click inside the column you wish to hide.

**To select adjacent columns:**

There are two methods to choose from when selecting several adjacent columns:

♦ Click and drag in the **Field Name** row (when the mouse pointer is a solid black arrow) across the columns.

Or

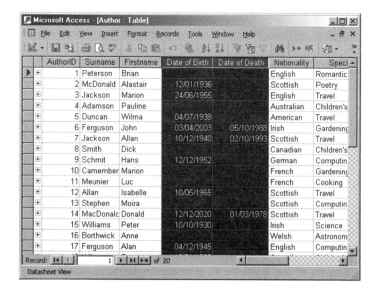

1 Select the first field by clicking anywhere in it.

2 Scroll through the columns until you can see the last column in the group you require.

3 Hold the [**Shift**] key down and click in the **Field Name** row at the top of the last column to be selected.

All the fields between the first and last column will be selected.

4 To hide the selected columns open the **Format** menu and choose **Hide Columns**.

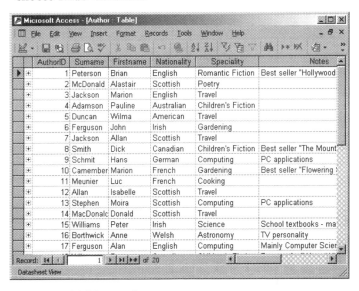

## Displaying hidden columns

When you want to display the columns again:

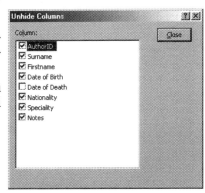

1 Choose **Unhide Columns...** from the **Format** menu.

2 Select the fields you want to display and click **Close**.

# 5.6 Freeze columns

When you freeze a column or columns, they become the leftmost columns in your table. Columns that are frozen do not scroll off the screen – they remain static while the other columns in your table scroll in and out of view.

**To freeze a column or columns:**

1  Select the column(s).

2  Open the **Format** menu.

3  Choose **Freeze columns**.

If the column(s) you choose are not at the left side of the table, they will be moved there.

If you need to freeze columns that are not adjacent to each other, select and freeze them one by one until you have built up the arrangement of frozen columns required. Once the columns are frozen you can scroll the other columns in and out of view as required – the frozen ones will remain at the left. On your screen, you will notice a dark vertical line between the frozen columns and unfrozen columns.

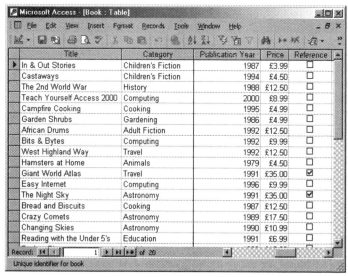

**To unfreeze a column or columns:**

♦  Choose **Unfreeze All Columns** from the **Format** menu.

The columns that are unfrozen remain to the left of the table – you have effectively moved the fields and placed the fields that were frozen at the beginning of the table.

### Closing the table

When you close your table, you will be asked if you want to save the changes to the layout of your table.

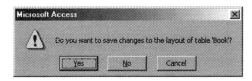

If you choose **Yes**, the new field order will be saved, if you choose **No** the fields will remain in the order they were before you froze them.

# 5.7 Preview and Print

### Print Preview

Before printing your table, it is recommended that you do a print Preview to check that it will look okay on the page. You can either select the table on the **Database** window OR display the table in Datasheet view to do this.

◆ Click the **Print Preview** tool 🔍 .

A preview of your datasheet will be displayed. Use the Print Preview toolbar to work with your table.

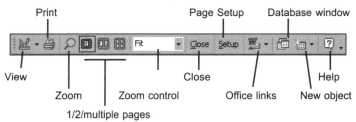

- To display a different view, click the **View** tool ▣ ▾.
- To send your table to the printer, click the **Print** tool 🖶.
- To zoom in on your datasheet, click the **Zoom** tool 🔍 – you click it to zoom out again (you can also zoom in and out if you place the mouse pointer over the preview page and click).
- The next three tools ▣ ▣▣ ▦ give you the option of viewing one, two or multiple pages at a time.
- The **Zoom Control** field [ Fit ▾ ] lets you set the percentage magnification of the zoom (the default options toggle the zoom between *100%* and *Fit* – which shows the whole page at a time).
- The [ Close ] tool returns you to Datasheet view, or to the **Database** window if you haven't gone into Datasheet view while previewing.
- The Setup tool [ Setup ] displays the Page Setup dialog box. If you need to change the margins or the orientation of your table before you print it, you can do so from here.

On the **Margins** tab of the dialog box, you can change the top, bottom, left or right margins. You can also specify whether or not you want to print headings, e.g. page number, table name (usually called Headers and Footers) at the top and bottom of each page.

On the **Page** tab, you can change the **Orientation** (portrait or landscape), the **Paper Size** and **Source** details, and the **Printer** details.

You can also display the Page Setup dialog box from Datasheet view:

1 Open your table in **Datasheet** view.

2 Select **Page Setup…** from the **File** menu.

## Print

You can print your datasheet from Print Preview or from the datasheet itself. To send one copy of the table to the printer:

- Click the **Print** tool 🖶 on either the Table Datasheet toolbar or the Print Preview toolbar.

## To select a group of records for printing:

* Click and drag down the row selector column (the grey column to the left of the records) in Datasheet view until you have highlighted the records required.

1 Choose **Print...** from the **File** menu.

2 Specify the options you require in the **Print** dialog box, e.g. *Selected Record(s)*.

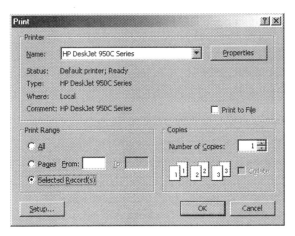

3 Click **OK**.

If you need to print more than one copy of your datasheet, or specific pages, rather than all the pages, you set these preferences through the **Print** dialog box.

You can also print a table directly from the Database window:

1 Select the table you want to print on the **Tables** list of the **Database** window.

2 Click the **Print** tool ⬛.

# Summary

In this chapter you have concentrated on a number of techniques that are useful when working with datasheets.

You have learnt how to:

- Change the field properties of existing fields.
- Rearrange the fields within your tables.
- Rename fields.
- Add new records to a table.
- Delete records from a table.
- Hide and unhide columns.
- Freeze and unfreeze columns.
- Preview your table prior to printing.
- Print your table.

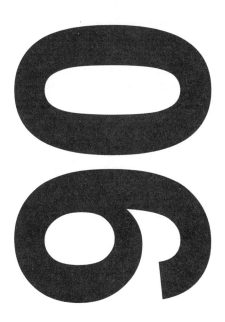

# 06

## forms design

**In this unit you will learn**

- how to design a form
- about some of the objects that you can use on a form
- how to add images to a form
- how to control the tab order
- about printing forms

# Aims of this chapter

In this chapter we will look at Forms design. Forms are not essential for data entry and edit, but they offer a much more user-friendly view of the data held in your tables than Datasheet view does. You can design your forms to look like the paper forms you use, or you can design them with a view to making your data entry and edit tasks easier.

AutoForm, the manual design of forms and Form Wizard will all be addressed in this chapter.

# 6.1 AutoForm

AutoForm was introduced in Chapter 4, where we discussed data entry and edit techniques.

You can generate a simple form based on any table or query in your database using AutoForm – see section 4.5 *Data entry in Form View* to recap on how you create an AutoForm. The screenshots on page 91 show Autoforms generated from the tables in the *Library* database.

* The autoform for the *Book* table is a simple columnar form.

* The autoform for the *Author* table displays the author details in a simple columnar layout, with a details of the books they have written listed in a *subform.*

* The *Category* table gives a similar form, with the category name followed by a list of the books in that category.

The design of your AutoForm can be edited using any forms design techniques discussed in this chapter – you can move the fields, resize them, change the labels, delete fields, and so on.

To edit the layout of your form you must take it into Design view by selecting *Design View* from the **View** options available.

When you leave a form which was created using AutoForm, you are given the option to save it. If you save the form it will be listed on the **Forms** list in the **Database** window.

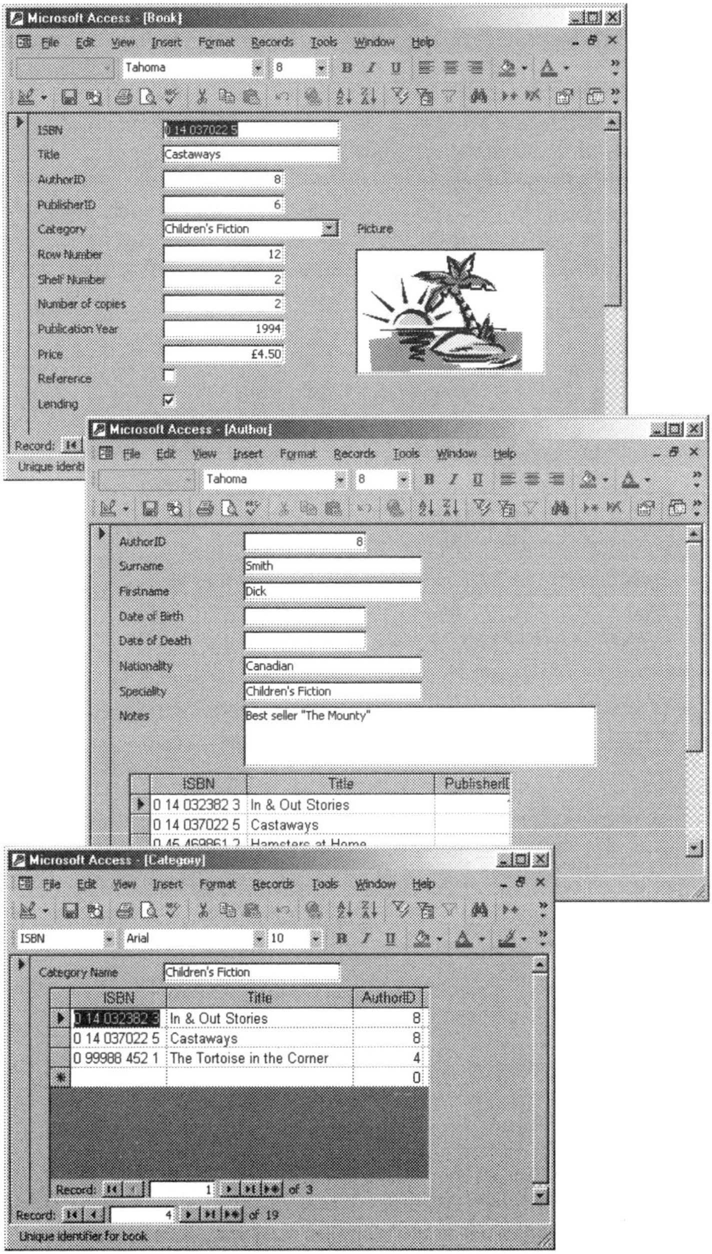


Autoforms of the Book, Author, and Category tables.

Even if you do not save your form, any records you added or edited will be stored in the table on which the form was based.

Experiment with AutoForm using the tables in your database.

# 6.2 Form Design

You can design your own form layout, selecting the fields you want to display and arranging them attractively on your screen.

We will design a simple form to display our *Publisher* details.

### Starting the Form design process

1 Select **Forms** on the Object bar in the **Database** window and click **New**.

2 At the **New Form** dialog box, select **Design View**.

3 Choose the *Publisher* table as the table or query from which the object's data comes.

4 Click **OK**.

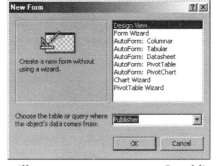

The **Form design** window will appear on your screen. In addition to the grid on which you design your form, there should also be a **Field List** displaying the field names from the table

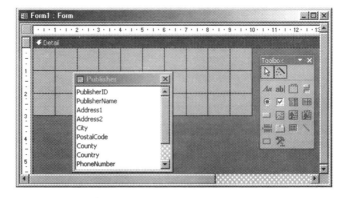

on which you are building the form, and a **Toolbox** that is used to help you design the form.

* If there is no Field List, click the **Field List** tool 🔳 to display it – this tool toggles the display of the Field List.

* If there is no Toolbox, click the **Toolbox** tool 🛠 to display it – this tool toggles the display of the Toolbox.

The Toolbox is actually a toolbar that can be moved around the screen like any other toolbar. If it is not docked and is obscuring your work, click and drag its title bar to move it to a new position, or drag the toolbar to a 'dock' at the top or the bottom of the screen (if you dock it right or left, not all the tools are visible).

## Form areas

The main areas in a form are the:

* **Detail** area
* **Form Header and Footer** area
* **Page Header and Footer** area.

The Detail area is the part of your form in which most of the detail from your table or query will be displayed.

The Form Header and Footer areas appear above and below the detail area for each record when you take your form back into Form view.

Form Headers and Footers are used for titles or instructions you wish to appear above and below each form.

* Open the **View** menu and choose **Form Header/Footer** to toggle the display of this area on and off.

The Page Headers and Footers appear at the top and bottom of each page, should you opt to print your form out. Page Headers would be used for main headings and column headings that you want to appear at the top of each printed page. The Page Footer is often used for page numbers, dates, or any other information you want to display at the foot of each page.

* Open the **View** menu and choose **Page Header/Footer** to toggle the display of this area on and off.

## Warning!

If you enter any data into the Form or Page Header or Footer areas, and then opt not to display the area, the data you entered will be lost.

In the form we are about to design, we need a Form Header/Footer area:

* Open the **View** menu and choose **Form Header/Footer** to display the area.

# 6.3 Labels

If you have instructions or headings to key into your form, you use the **Label** tool. We need a heading in our Form Header area – 'Book Publishers'.

1 Click the **Label** tool ![Label tool icon].

2 Move the mouse pointer into the form header area (notice the mouse pointer shape ⁺A).

3 Click and drag in the **Form Header** area to draw a rectangle where you want your heading to go.

4 Let go the mouse – the insertion point is inside the label field.

5 Key in your heading.

6 Click anywhere outside the label field.

Create another label underneath the one you have just made. This one should contain the text:

Publisher name and address details

If you think the Form Header area is not deep enough for this label, you can resize it by clicking and dragging the bottom edge of the header area (the mouse pointer will change to a black double headed arrow when you are in the correct place). The header area will also deepen automatically if you enter a label field too deep for its current size.

Your design should be similar to the one on the next page.

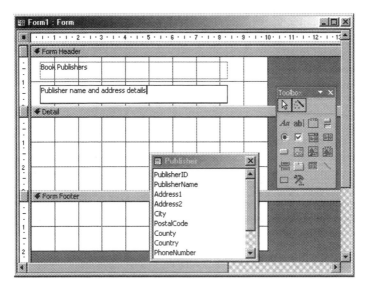

## 6.4 Formatting fields

The fields you have added can be moved, resized, formatted or deleted – so it is not critical that you get everything right first time.

To change the field attributes, you must select the field you want to work on.

◆ Click on the *Book Publishers* title to select it.

You will notice that a selected field has 'handles' around it – one in each corner and one half way along each side.

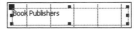

◆ To resize a field, click and drag a handle in the direction you wish the field to resize to.

◆ To move a field, position the mouse pointer over the edge of the field (not over a handle) and click and drag – the mouse pointer looks like a hand when you are in the correct place.

◆ To delete a field, select it, then press the [**Delete**] key.

Try making the *Book Publishers* heading font style Arial, font size 20, bold and text colour red! Now make the *Publisher name and address details* bold, italic and font size 12.

- To change the font size, colour, toggle bold, italics, underline, etc. experiment with the options on the **Formatting** toolbar when the field is selected.

If the toolbar is not displayed, choose **Toolbars** from the **View** menu then select **Formatting** (**Form/Report**)

If the data is too large for the field, resize the field as necessary. Your design should look something like the example below.

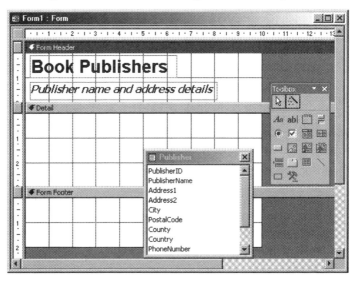

In the detail area of our form, we want to display the data held in the Publishers table – name, phone number, address, and so on.

- Deepen the **Detail** area ready for the fields you are about to insert into it. You can click and drag its bottom edge to resize it.

If you want your form to be wider, you can click and drag the rightmost edge of it to resize it.

## 6.5 Text boxes

To set up the design for the detail area we have to click and drag the fields required from the Field List onto the Detail area of our form. Once the fields are in the Detail area, we can position them, resize and format them as necessary. The fields we drag from the field list to the form are displayed as *text boxes*.

* Click and drag the *Publisher Name* field from the **Field List** and drop it on the detail area of your form.

You will notice that fields from the Field List consist of two parts – the leftmost part is the field label (either the field name or the caption if you entered one in the field properties), the rightmost part will display the actual data held in the field when you return to Form view.

*Both* components of the field are selected – if you move or delete the field the whole thing will be affected.

You can move either side of the field independently. Simply drag the large selection handle at the top left of each part when the field is selected.

* Place the *PublisherID* field next to the *PublisherName* one. Your form should now look similar to the one below.

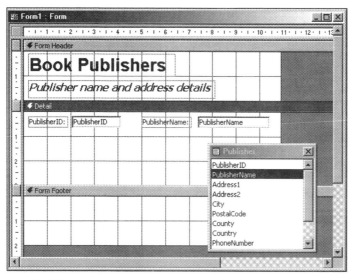

* Format the label of each field (the left part) to be font size 10 and bold – click on the leftmost part to select it, then use the Formatting toolbar to apply the formats required.

We are now ready to arrange the address details. This time, we want only one heading *Address* for all the individual address fields we will insert.

◆ Use the **Label** tool 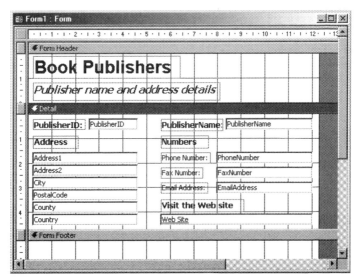 and enter a label that says '*Address*' below the *PublisherName* field.

Arranged under this, we want the *Address1*, *Address2*, *City*, *County*, *Postalcode* and *Country* fields. However, as we already have an *Address* label, we do not require the individual field labels – so we can delete them.

1 Click and drag your first field over – probably *Address1*. To delete the label (field name or caption), select the leftmost part of the field (click on it) and press [**Delete**] on your keyboard. The label should disappear but the rightmost part should remain.

2 Do the same with the other address fields, and arrange them attractively on your form.

3 Insert the *Phone, Fax, e-mail and Web site* fields to the right of the address detail (use labels as you wish to enhance the layout).

4 We don't need the Form Footer area on this form – click and drag its bottom edge up until it disappears.

Your form should be similar to the one below.

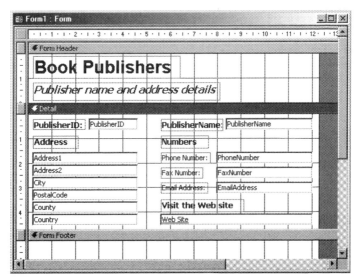

5 Click the **Save** tool on the Form Design toolbar to save your form. At the **Save As** dialog box, give your form a suitable name and click **OK**.

6 Take your form through into Form view to see how it looks. It should be similar to the one below.

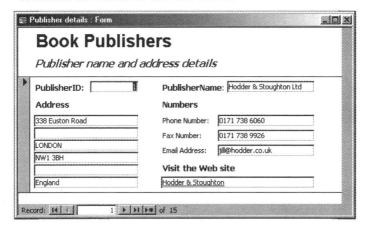

When you close your form, you will find its name displayed on the Forms list in the Database window.

# 6.6 Form Wizard

In addition to the manual design of forms, you could try out the Form Wizard when you need to design a form. The wizard takes you through the forms design process step by step, asking you questions on the way.

We are going to design a form displaying the *ISBN*, *Title* and *Category* fields from the *Book* table, the *AuthorName* details from the *Author* table, and the *PublisherName* from the *Publisher* table.

**To start creating your form using Form Wizard:**

1 Select **Forms** on the Objects bar in the **Database** window.

2  Click **New**.

3  At the **New Form** dialog box, choose **Form Wizard** and click **OK**.

At the first **Form Wizard** dialog box, select a table or query from which you want to include fields (you can include fields from more than one table or query on your form).

4  Choose the *Book* table and move the *ISBN*, *Title* and *Category Name* fields from the **Available fields list:** over into the **Selected fields:** list.

5  Select the *Author* table from the **Tables/Queries** list and add the *Firstname* and *Surname* fields.

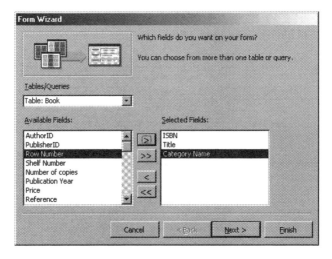

| Working in a wizard | |
|---|---|
| To move on to the next step | Click  Next > |
| To go back a step | Click  < Back |
| To exit the wizard without creating a form | Click  Cancel |
| To create a form using the default options | Click  Finish |

6  Finally, select the *Publisher* table from the **Tables/Queries** list and add the *PublisherName* field.

The completed dialog box should look like this:

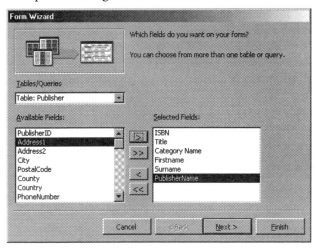

Now move on to the next step.

7 Select the option to use when viewing your data. In this example, choose **By Book**, and **Single** form. Click **Next**.

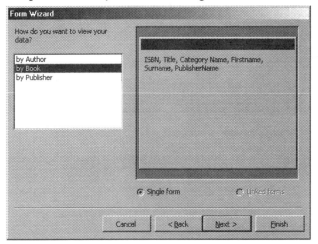

8 Choose the layout you want to use for your form – **Columnar** in this example – and click **Next**.

At the next step you can choose the style of your forms. The style determines the colours and design layout. Pick one and move on to the next step.

When you reach the checkered flag you are at the last step in the wizard.

9  Give your form a name (either accept the one suggested or key in your own – this name will appear on the **Forms** list in the **Database** window).

10 Select **Open the form to view or enter information** and click **Finish**.

Your form should look something like this:

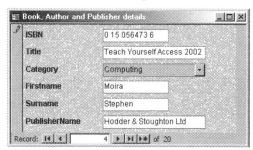

You can tab through the fields in your record using the [**Tab**] key, and move between records using the navigation buttons at the bottom of the form.

When you close your form, you will find it on the **Forms** list in the **Database** window.

If you would like your data displayed in a summary form, e.g. a list of all the books you have from each publisher, the Form Wizard can easily help you design the form required for this.

**Further work with a wizard**

Work through the Form Wizard again selecting the following fields for your form. (You can include the *PublisherID* and/or *AuthorID* if you want to.)

> *Publisher* table:  *PublisherName*
>
> *Book* table:  *ISBN*, *Title* and *Category Name*
>
> *Author* table:  *Firstname* and *Surname*

1  When you get to the step where you are asked to select the option you want to use when viewing your data – choose **By Publisher**.

2 Select the **Form with subforms** option – the *Publisher* form will have a subform within it listing the book details.

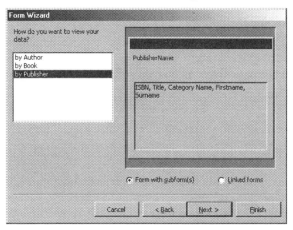

3 At the next step choose the layout you want for your subform (tabular or datasheet).

4 Continue working through the Wizard, specifying the style and names you want to use for your forms (either accept the default ones, or amend them to your liking). These form names will be displayed on the **Forms** list in the **Database** window.

5 At the checkered flag, choose **Open the form to view or enter information** and click **Finish**.

Two forms will be generated – your main form, the publisher one, and the book subform.

◆ Looking at your form you can use the lower set of navigation buttons to move from one publisher record to another.

◆ If you have a long list of books you can use the upper set of navigation buttons to move through the books in the list.

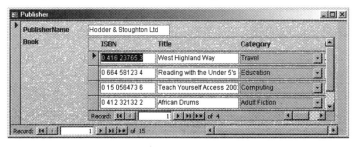

If you take the form through into Design view, you can see how this was set up.

The *PublisherID* (if included) and *PublisherName* fields, are text boxes.

The lower section is a subform/subreport field. A subform field can display data from an existing table, query or form. The subform must be identified as the source of the data that will be displayed in that area of your main form. This is set up in the property options for that field.

* To view the property options, select the *Subform* field – either click on it or select it from the Objects list on the Formatting (Form/Report) toolbar – and click the **Properties** tool 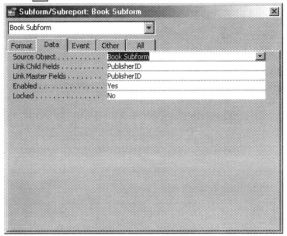 on the **Form Design** toolbar.

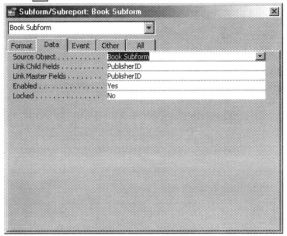

The subform/subreport property options are displayed in a dialog box. The **Data** tab shows the source of the data and the linking fields.

* Close the dialog box when you have finished.

## 6.7 Combo boxes and List boxes

Combo boxes and List boxes can be used when you have a limited list of options to choose from. Using them can help ensure accurate data entry as the user can select the entry rather than type it in. When you specify a LookUp field in the data type of a table a Combo box is created automatically in the table and when you add the field to a form.

We could use a Combo box or a List box for the *Country* field in the *Publishers* details form. The publishers that we deal with are all from England, Scotland and the USA.

## Combo box

To insert a Combo box field for *Country*, take the Publisher details form into Design view and delete the *Country* field.

1 Click the **Combo box** tool 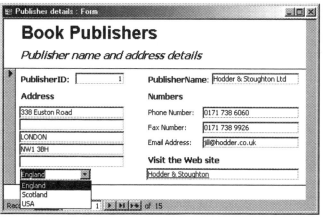 on the Toolbox.

2 Drag the field that you wish to use from the field list onto your form – *Country* in this example.

3 Select *I will type in the values that I want* and click **Next**.

4 Specify the number of columns in the box – we only need one.

5 Enter the possible values for the Combo box – 'England', 'Scotland' and 'USA'.

6 Drag the edge of the column to set its width and click **Next**.

7 Select the field to store the Combo box value in – *Country* should be suggested – and click **Next**.

8 Give the Combo box a label – accept the default or set your own.

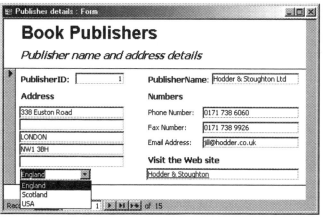

9 Click **Finish**.

10 Resize and position the Combo box as needed.

## List boxes

List boxes are set up in exactly the same way as a Combo box, just start with the **List box** tool 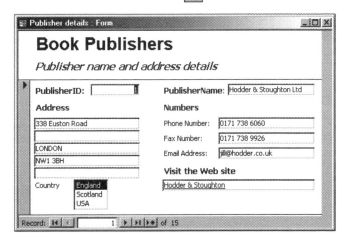.

# 6.8 Checkboxes and buttons

If you simply drag a Yes/No field onto a form, it will be displayed as a Checkbox, but Yes/No fields can also be displayed as Toggle buttons or Option buttons. It is conventional to use Checkboxes or Toggle buttons for Yes/No indicators. Option buttons are normally associated with groups of options, from which only one can be selected.

**To display a Yes/No field as a Toggle button:**

1 Click the **Toggle button** tool .

2 Drag the field from the field list onto your form.

3 With the field selected, click the **Properties** tool and enter a suitable caption for the button.

4 Close the **Properties** dialog box.

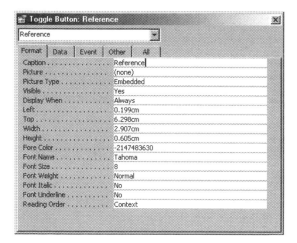

To display a Yes/No field as an Option button:

1 Click the **Option button** tool ⦿.

2 Drag the field from the field list onto your form and position it as required.

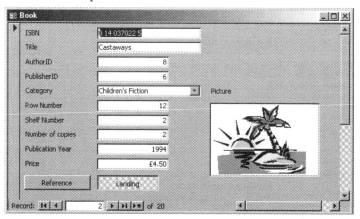

# 6.9 Option group

Option groups are useful when you have a limited number of options, from which you can select one. We could use a group for the *Shelf Number* in the *Book* form. Open the *Book* form in Design view and delete the *Shelf Number* field (you might want to rearrange some of the fields to make room for the group).

1  Click the **Option group** tool 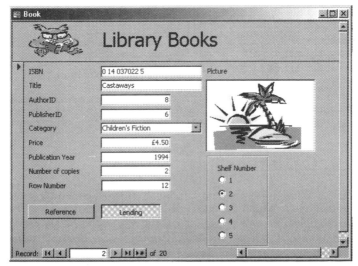.

2  Drag the field from the field list onto the form.

•  Work through the wizard, clicking **Next** after each step.

3  Insert the **Label name** for each option button.

4  Specify the default choice if you wish.

5  Edit the **Values** if necessary – the values will be stored in the underlying table.

6  Indicate the field where the value will be stored.

7  Set the display options.

8  Edit the Option group caption if necessary.

9  Click **Finish**.

Move/resize the Option group as required.

## 6.10  Inserting images

You can easily insert an image onto a form (or report).

1  Display the form area that you want the image on.

2  Click the **Image** tool.

3  Drag on the form to set the size and position for the image.

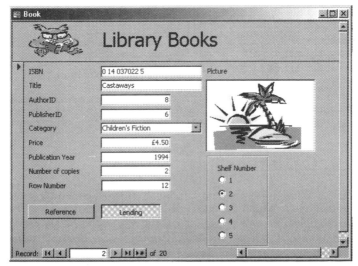

4   Locate the picture (browse through your drives and folders).
Move/resize the image as required.

## Calculations

You can perform calculations on a form, as in queries, using
the operators + (add), - (minus), * (multiply) and / (divide).
Calculations must be placed in a Text box.

1   Create a Text box on your form.

2   Replace the left-hand side text with the label you want
   your field to have.

3   Enter the formula required in the right-hand side.

4   Format the right-hand side as required, e.g. currency,
   decimal places (in the Property options for the field).

5   Go into Form View to see the results.

# 6.11  Command buttons

Command buttons perform actions such as printing a form,
finding a record of applying a filter.

1   Click the **Command button** tool ▣.

2   Click where you want the button on the form.

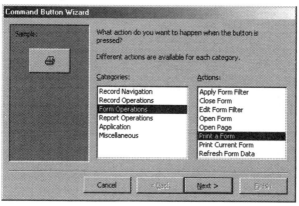

3 Select the **Category** and **Action**.

4 Work through the steps of the Command button Wizard, setting options as required.

5 Click **Finish**.

## 6.12 Tab control

Some forms contain many fields and/or text e.g. instructions. With these you can use separate pages in the Tab control to display different areas of the information on your form.

1 Click the **Tab control** tool 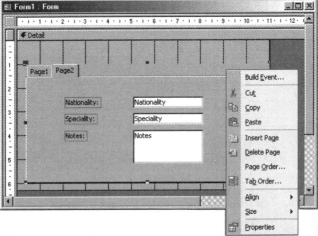.

2 Click and drag in the Detail area to place the Tab control.

3 Add the fields required on page 1.

4 Select the page 2 tab and add its fields.

**To add or delete pages:**

1 Click on the tab of the page you wish to insert after, or display the page to delete.

2 Right-click on the field and select **Insert page** or **Delete page** as required.

**To change page order:**

1 Right-click on the field and click **Page Order...**

2  Select the page and click **Move Up** or **Move Down** as necessary.

◆  Pages can be renamed by editing the **Name** on the **Other** tab of their **Properties** sheet.

---

## Tab order

When designing a form you will probably move you fields around and change their order several times before you are finally satisfied with the form layout. As a result of this, you may find that when you press **[Tab]** to move from field to field in Form view, you jump around all over the place. When this happens, you should reset the Tab order to give a more logical progression through the form.

In Design View, select Tab Order from the View menu. Drag the fields into the order you wish to tab through them, or Select Auto Order to tab through them in the order that they appear on the form.

---

# 6.13  Printing forms

Forms are usually used for data entry and edit. There may be times when you want to print your forms out – you could perhaps print out an empty form to send to someone for manual completion.

If you want to print out a form, you can do so using similar techniques to those used when printing out a datasheet.

1  Select the form you want to print on the **Forms** tab in the **Database** window.

2  Click the **Print Preview** tool to preview the form, or click the **Print** tool to print out a copy.

Or

◆  Open the form in Form view, and preview and print from there.

Access will fit as many forms as possible on the page size you have selected, so depending on the size of your form, you may have one or several forms printed out on the same sheet.

# Summary

In this chapter we have looked at different ways of designing your own forms. You have learnt how to:

+ Create an AutoForm.

+ Set up a simple form manually.

+ Switch headers and footers on and off.

+ Set up labels and text boxes.

+ Use Form Wizard to generate forms for you.

+ Use Combo and List boxes.

+ Use Checkboxes and buttons in your forms.

+ Use the Wizard to set up Option groups.

+ Insert images into your form.

+ Use Command buttons.

+ Control the Tab order on forms.

+ Print your forms.

# 07

## sort, filter and query

**In this unit you will learn**

- about simple and multi-level sorts
- how to find data
- about filtering records from tables
- about select and parameter queries
- about calculations in queries

# Aims of this chapter

In this chapter, you will learn how to sort the records in your tables into the required order, find records and filter the records to display those that meet specific criteria. You will also learn how to create expressions to extract records that meet specific criteria from your table.

The techniques discussed in this chapter can be used on your tables in Datasheet view or in Form view.

## 7.1 Simple sort

It is very easy to sort the records in your table on a single field.

1 Open the table you are going to sort.
2 Place the insertion point anywhere within the field you want to sort the records on.
3 Click the **Sort Ascending** 📶 or **Sort Descending** 📶 tool.

* To sort the records in the *Book* table in ascending order on the *Title* field, open the *Book* table, place the insertion point anywhere within the *Title* field, and click the **Sort Ascending** tool.

The *Book* table, with the records sorted into ascending order on the *Title* field, is displayed below.

| ISBN | Title | Category | AuthorID | PublisherID | Row N |
|------|-------|----------|----------|-------------|-------|
| 0 412 32132 2 | African Drums | Adult Fiction | 14 | 1 | |
| 0 412 46512 1 | Bits & Bytes | Computing | 13 | 2 | |
| 0 563 49124 5 | Bread and Biscuits | Cooking | 11 | 7 | |
| 0 345 12342 3 | Campfire Cooking | Cooking | 20 | 8 | |
| 0 14 037022 5 | Castaways | Children's Fiction | 8 | 6 | |
| 0 587 39561 0 | Changing Skies | Astronomy | 16 | 2 | |
| 0 576 26111 0 | Crazy Comets | Astronomy | 15 | 13 | |
| 0 482 31456 1 | Easy Internet | Computing | 17 | 2 | |
| 0 34532 375 1 | Garden Shrubs | Gardening | 6 | 8 | |
| 0 465 77654 3 | Giant World Atlas | Travel | 20 | 13 | |
| 0 45 469861 2 | Hamsters at Home | Animals | 8 | 6 | |
| 0 14 032382 3 | In & Out Stories | Children's Fiction | 8 | 11 | |
| 0 85234 432 6 | Outdoor Adventures | Travel | 12 | 10 | |
| 0 758 34512 1 | Perfect Pizzas | Cooking | 11 | 15 | |
| 0 664 58123 4 | Reading with the Under 5's | Education | 8 | 1 | |
| 0 15 056473 6 | Teach Yourself Access 2002 | Computing | 13 | 1 | |
| 0 14 930654 7 | The 2nd World War | History | 3 | 14 | |
| 0 55345 456 2 | The Night Sky | Astronomy | 2 | 13 | |
| 0 99988 452 1 | The Tortoise in the Corner | Children's Fiction | 4 | 6 | |
| 0 416 23765 3 | West Highland Way | Travel | 7 | 1 | |

Record: 1 of 20

## Saving changes

When you close a table that you have sorted, you will be asked if you want to save the changes.

To save the records in the new, sorted order, choose **Yes**.

# 7.2 Multi-level sort

If you want to sort your table on several fields, you must set up your sort requirements in the **Filter** dialog box.

You might want to sort your *Book* table into ascending order on *Category Name*, and within each category you might want the books sorted into ascending order on *Title*. If necessary, open your *Book* table to try this out.

1  From the **Records** menu, select **Filter, Advanced Filter/ Sort...**

2  In the upper half of the **Filter** dialog box the field list of the current table is displayed. Scroll through the list until you see your main sort field – in our case *Category Name*.

3  Double click on the field name – the field name will appear in the first empty column of the field row in the lower pane.

4  Place the insertion point in the **Sort** row below the field name (you can move from pane to pane by pressing the [**F6**] key on

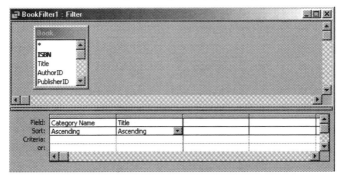

your keyboard, or use your mouse). Either type the letter **a** to select **Ascending** order, or display the options available (click the **drop-down arrow**) and choose **Ascending**.

5  Return to the upper pane and double click on the field required for your second level sort – *Title* in our case. In the lower pane set the sort order to **Ascending**.

6  Once you have set up the options required, click the **Apply Filter** tool ▼ to display your records in the new order.

| ISBN | Title | Category | AuthorID | PublisherID | Row Numb |
|------|-------|----------|----------|-------------|----------|
| 0 412 32132 2 | African Drums | Adult Fiction | 14 | 1 | |
| 0 45 469861 2 | Hamsters at Home | Animals | 8 | 6 | |
| 0 587 39561 0 | Changing Skies | Astronomy | 16 | 2 | |
| 0 576 26111 2 | Crazy Comets | Astronomy | 15 | 13 | |
| 0 55345 456 2 | The Night Sky | Astronomy | 2 | 13 | |
| 0 14 037022 5 | Castaways | Children's Fiction | 8 | 6 | |
| 0 14 032382 3 | In & Out Stories | Children's Fiction | 8 | 11 | |
| 0 99988 452 1 | The Tortoise in the Corner | Children's Fiction | 4 | 6 | |
| 0 412 46512 1 | Bits & Bytes | Computing | 13 | 2 | |
| 0 482 31456 1 | Easy Internet | Computing | 17 | 2 | |
| 0 15 056473 6 | Teach Yourself Access 2002 | Computing | 13 | 1 | |
| 0 563 49124 5 | Bread and Biscuits | Cooking | 11 | 7 | |
| 0 345 12342 3 | Campfire Cooking | Cooking | 20 | 8 | |
| 0 758 34512 1 | Perfect Pizzas | Cooking | 11 | 15 | |
| 0 664 58123 4 | Reading with the Under 5's | Education | 8 | 1 | |
| 0 34532 375 1 | Garden Shrubs | Gardening | 6 | 8 | |
| 0 14 930654 7 | The 2nd World War | History | 3 | 14 | |
| 0 465 77654 3 | Giant World Atlas | Travel | 20 | 13 | |
| 0 85234 432 6 | Outdoor Adventures | Travel | 12 | 10 | |
| 0 416 23765 3 | West Highland Way | Travel | 7 | 1 | |
| * | | | 0 | 0 | |

Records: ◄ ◄ | 1 | ► ►I ►* of 20

### Saving sorted records separately

If you do not want to overwrite the original record order, but you want to save the sort options you have set up for future use, you can save the options as a Query. You must return to the **Filter** dialog box to do this (**Records, Filter, Advanced Filter/Sort…**).

♦  Click the **Filter** button on the taskbar

Or

♦  Click the **Save As Query** 💾 tool on the Filter/Sort toolbar. Give your query a suitable name – *Sorted on Category then Title* – and click **OK**.

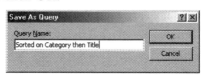

Your query will appear on the **Queries** list in the **Database** window.

Your filter criteria have been saved as a Query. When you open the query from the **Database** window, it appears in a **Select Query** window, rather than the **Filter** window in which it was designed.

# 7.3 Find

To locate a record in your table, you can use the navigation buttons at the bottom of your datasheet or form, or go to a specific record by typing its number in the number field within the navigation buttons and pressing [**Enter**].

If you have a lot of records in your table, the Find function can provide a quick way of locating a specific record.

Try locating a book in a particular category:

1 Place the insertion point anywhere within the *Category* field in the *Book* table.
2 Click the **Find** tool 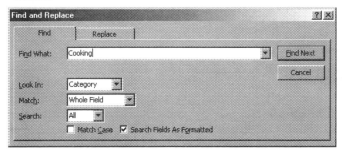.
3 At the **Find** dialog box, enter the detail you are looking for – *Cooking* in this example.
4 Edit the other fields as necessary.
5 Click **Find Next** to start the search or look for another match.

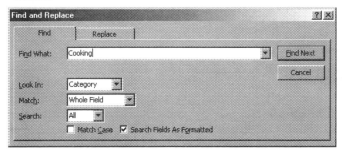

6 Close the dialog box once you have found your record.

# 7.4 Filter

There will be times when you want to display a specific group of records from your table – a list of American authors, or authors who specialize in travel books for example. This is done by *filtering* the records. You can filter your records **By Selection** or **By Form**.

## Filter By Selection

Try filtering the *Author* table to display those of a specific nationality.

1   Open the *Author* table.

2   Position the insertion point in the field of a record that has the criteria you are looking for – if you are looking for American authors, position the insertion field within the *Nationality* field, in a record where the author is American.

3   Click the **Filter By Selection** tool ![icon].

A subset of the records within your table will be displayed.

4   You can filter your filtered list using the same technique – narrowing down your list of records as you go, e.g. to display those who specialize in travel books.

5   To display all your records again, click the **Remove Filter** tool ![icon].

The main limitation with filtering is that you can specify only **one** criterion per field, e.g. you can track down all American authors, but not all American and Scottish authors at the same time.

## Filter By Form

When you **Filter By Form**, you can specify multiple criteria at the one time (unlike **Filter By Selection** where you narrow down your search one criterion at a time). You can also specify different criteria in any one field.

In our *Author* table we could look for Scottish authors who specialize in Travel, or Scottish AND American authors who specialize in Travel.

1  Click the **Filter By Form** tool ▣.

You are presented with an empty record.

As you move from field to field, you will notice that each behaves like a Combo Box in which you can display a list of options.

2  Enter your first set of criteria on the **Look for** tab. In the *Nationality* field, choose **Scottish** from the list, and in the *Speciality* field choose **Travel** from the list.

3  If you wish to set up another set of criteria, click on the first **Or** tab and enter the next set, e.g. look for American authors who specialize in Travel, or English authors specializing in Romantic Fiction.

4  Continue until all criteria have been set up.

5  Click the **Apply Filter** tool ▣ – all records meeting the criteria specified will be displayed.

6  To display all your records again, click **Remove Filter** ▣.

# 7.5  Querying more than one table

In the examples up until now, we have sorted and filtered records within one table. There will be times when you need to collect the data you require from several tables, and sort or filter that data.

When working across several tables, you must set up a Query from the **Database** window.

We will set up a Query to display *Book Title*, *Author*, *Publisher* and *Year Published* data.

If you have a table open, close it and return to the **Database** window.

1  At the **Database** window, select **Queries** in the Objects bar and click ▣New.

2  At the **New Query** dialog box, choose **Design View** and click **OK**.

Or

♦  Double-click ▣ Create query in Design view to display the **Select Query** dialog box.

3 You will arrive at the **Select Query** dialog box. The **Show Table** window should be open, listing the tables in your database – if it is not, click the **Show Table** tool 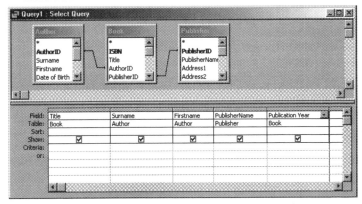 to display the list.

4 Add the *Author* table, *Book* table and *Publisher* table to the **Select Query** dialog box.

5 Close the **Show Table** window.

6 You will notice some extra rows in the lower pane of the **Select Query** dialog box.

♦ The **Table** row displays the name of the table from which a field is taken.

♦ The **Show** row indicates whether or not a selected field will be displayed in the result – a tick in the box means the field detail will be displayed, no tick means the detail will not be displayed. The default for all fields is that the detail will be displayed.

7 Select the fields you want, in the order you want them to appear, from the tables – double click on the names in the field lists.

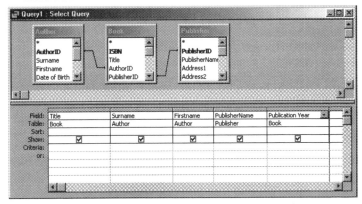

You will need the:

♦ *Title* from the *Book* table

♦ *Surname* and *Firstname* from the *Author* table

♦ *PublisherName* from the *Publisher* table

♦ *Publication year* from the *Book* table.

8 Run the query. Click the **Run** tool 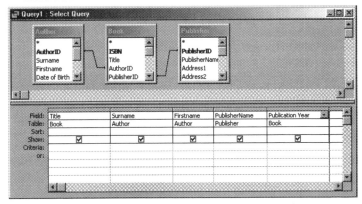 and note the results.

| Title | Surname | Firstname | PublisherName | Publication Year |
|---|---|---|---|---|
| In & Out Stories | Smith | Dick | Scrambler Publication Ltd | 1987 |
| Castaways | Smith | Dick | Arrows Publications | 1994 |
| The 2nd World War | Jackson | Marion | Carling & Sons plc | 1988 |
| Teach Yourself Access 2002 | Stephen | Moira | Hodder & Stoughton Ltd | 2000 |
| Campfire Cooking | Watson | George | Beaver Books Ltd | 1995 |
| Garden Shrubs | Ferguson | John | Beaver Books Ltd | 1986 |
| African Drums | MacDonald | Donald | Hodder & Stoughton Ltd | 1992 |
| Bits & Bytes | Stephen | Moira | Borthwick-Henderson | 1992 |
| West Highland Way | Jackson | Allan | Hodder & Stoughton Ltd | 1992 |
| Hamsters at Home | Smith | Dick | Arrows Publications | 1979 |
| Giant World Atlas | Watson | George | Outreach College Press | 1991 |
| Easy Internet | Ferguson | Alan | Borthwick-Henderson | 1996 |
| The Night Sky | McDonald | Alastair | Outreach College Press | 1991 |
| Bread and Biscuits | Meunier | Luc | Harry Cousin Ltd | 1987 |
| Crazy Comets | Williams | Peter | Outreach College Press | 1989 |

*Query1 : Select Query*

Record: 1 of 20

The selected fields from *all* your records are displayed.

9 Save your query – you could call it something like, *Title, Author and Publisher details.*

10 Close your Query – you will find it on the **Queries** list in the **Database** window.

As you try out the following examples, save any queries you want to keep.

# 7.6 Select Queries

If you want a subset of your records, you must specify any criteria you want to base your selected records on in the **Select Query** dialog box. The criteria are specified through expressions that you key into the criteria rows. When entering expressions there are one or two rules you should keep in mind.

If you want to look for multiple criteria within the same record, the criteria are entered on the same row. If you wanted a list of all the books published by Hodder & Stoughton, you would enter '*Hodder & Stoughton Ltd*' in the *PublisherName* column in the criteria row.

However, if you wanted a list of all the books published by Hodder & Stoughton Ltd in 1992, you would enter **Hodder & Stoughton Ltd** in the *PublisherName* column and **1992** in the *Publication Year* column on the same criteria row.

When you enter criteria in different cells in the same row, Access uses the **And** operator. It looks for all the conditions being met before returning the record details. If you enter criteria in cells in different criteria rows, Access uses the **Or** operator.

Experiment with different criteria using your tables.

1 Create a new Query in Design View.

2 Add the *Book*, *Author* and *Publisher* tables to the **Select Query** window.

3 Select the fields you want, in the order you want them to appear – you can use the same ones as in the previous example:

♦ *Title* from the *Book* table

♦ *Surname* and *Firstname* from the *Author* table

♦ *PublisherName* from the *Publisher* table

♦ *Publication Year* from the *Book* table.

# 7.7 Or conditions

This time, we want our books in ascending order on the Title field, but we only want to show the books we have from the publishers Hodder & Stoughton Ltd and those from Borthwick-Henderson Ltd. We have also decided not to display the details in the Publication year column.

1 Set the sort order required in the Title column

2 In the *PublisherName* column, enter '*Hodder & Stoughton Ltd*' in the first criteria row and '*Borthwick-Henderson Ltd*' in the next criteria row – Access will return records that have **Hodder & Stoughton Ltd** OR **Borthwick-Henderson Ltd** in the *PublisherName* field.

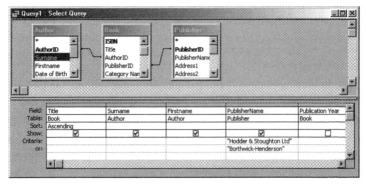

| Field: | Title | Surname | Firstname | PublisherName | Publication Year |
|--------|-------|---------|-----------|---------------|------------------|
| Table: | Book | Author | Author | Publisher | Book |
| Sort: | Ascending | | | | |
| Show: | ☑ | ☑ | ☑ | ☑ | ☐ |
| Criteria: | | | | "Hodder & Stoughton Ltd" | |
| or: | | | | "Borthwick-Henderson" | |

3 Deselect the **Show** checkbox in the *Publication Year* column as we do not want this column displayed in the result.

4 Run your query – click the **Run** tool ▮ – and note the results.

| Title | Surname | Firstname | PublisherName |
|-------|---------|-----------|---------------|
| African Drums | MacDonald | Donald | Hodder & Stoughton Ltd |
| Bits & Bytes | Stephen | Moira | Borthwick-Henderson |
| Changing Skies | Borthwick | Anne | Borthwick-Henderson |
| Easy Internet | Ferguson | Alan | Borthwick-Henderson |
| Reading with the Under 5's | Smith | Dick | Hodder & Stoughton Ltd |
| Teach Yourself Access 2002 | Stephen | Moira | Hodder & Stoughton Ltd |
| West Highland Way | Jackson | Allan | Hodder & Stoughton Ltd |

Record: 14 ◀ 1 ▶ ▶I ▶* of 7

The book titles should be in ascending order, the author name and publisher name are displayed – but only for the publishers specified in the criteria rows. The year of publication is not displayed.

## 7.8 And conditions

This time try to get a list of all the books published by Hodder & Stoughton Ltd in 1992.

1 Enter '*Hodder & Stoughton Ltd*' in the *PublisherName* and '*1992*' in the *Publication Year* column of the first criteria row.

2 Run your query – click the **Run** tool ▮.

Access will return details for records where both criteria are met in the same record – those that have **Hodder & Stoughton Ltd** in the *PublisherName* field AND **1992** in the *Publication Year* column.

## 7.9 Comparison operators

When you enter an expression in the **Criteria** row, as in the examples in sections 7.7 and 7.8, Access assumes that you mean to use the comparison operator =, i.e. you are looking for records where the text or value in the corresponding field in the datasheet is equal to the text or value that you have entered in the **Criteria** row in the **Query Design** grid.

There will be times when you wish to extract records using different comparison operators. If you don't mean 'equals' you must enter the appropriate operator into your expression in the Criteria row.

You can identify the range required using the following operators:

| < | Less than |
|---|---|
| > | More than |
| <= | Less than or equal to |
| >= | More than or equal to |
| <> | Not equal to |
| Between...And... | Between the first and the last value entered (including the values) |

To get a list of books by authors whose surname began with the letter **M** through to the end of the alphabet, you would enter >**M** in the criteria row of the *Surname* column.

If you want a list of books published before 1994, you would enter <**1994** in the criteria row in the *Publication Year* column.

To get a list of all the books published in 1992, 1993, 1994, 1995 and 1996 you would enter **Between 1992 And 1996** in the criteria row of the *Publication Year* column.

The on-line help will give you other examples of expressions you can experiment with.

# 7.10  Wild card characters

When specifying your criteria you can use 'wild card' characters to represent either individual characters or a string of characters. The wild card characters are:

\*       which can be used to represent a string of characters or

?       which can be used to represent a single character.

For example, if you wanted a list of all the publishers in your database with a postcode of NW1 you could use the \* wild card to represent the second part of the postcode so that its detail didn't matter.

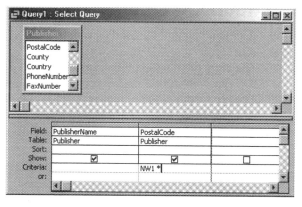

Enter NW1* into the criteria row for the Postcode field. When you leave the cell, the NW1* changes to read Like "NW1*". All records that have a postcode beginning with NW1 will be returned when you run the query.

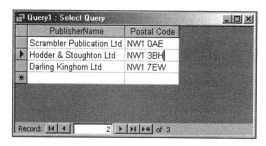

If you wanted a list of all books that had the word 'Cooking' in the title, but sometimes the word appeared at the beginning, e.g. *Cooking for Kids*, or in the middle, e.g. *Indian Cooking for Beginners* or at the end, e.g. *Party Cooking*, the wild cards can help you get a complete list. Entering *Cooking* in the criteria row would do the trick!

Single letters that may vary can be represented using the ?. If you wanted to find a particular author in your list, but you couldn't remember whether the surname was Wilson or Wilton, you could enter **\*Wil?on\*** in the criteria row.

# 7.11 Parameter Queries

There may be times when you run the same query regularly, but you need to change the criteria each time. Instead of entering the criteria into the Design view for the query, you can enter a *prompt* that will appear on the screen requesting your input each time you run the query.

You could set up a query to list the books written by a specific author with a prompt to ask for the author name each time the query is run.

1 In the criteria row, in the *Surname* column enter the prompt you wish to appear when the query is run: '*[Enter Surname]*'

2 Enter a prompt in the *Firstname* column: '*[Enter Firstname]*'

The prompts *must* be included within [**square brackets**], and they *cannot* consist of just the field name, although the field name may be included within the prompt – '*[Surname]*' won't work, but '*[Enter Surname]*' will!

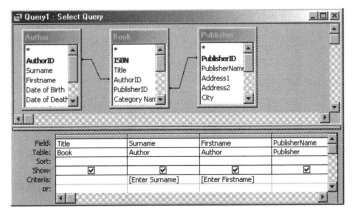

3 Run the query ![ ! ].

4 Enter the *Surname* detail, and click **OK**.

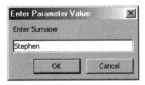

5 Likewise, enter the *Firstname* detail, and click **OK**.

The results will be displayed on your screen.

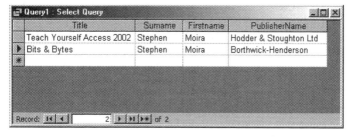

6   Save this Query – you could call it *Prompt for author name.*

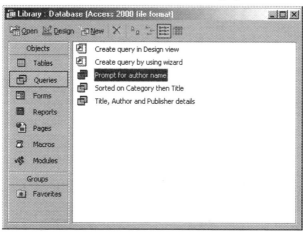

You will find the queries you have saved listed under **Queries** tab in the **Database** window.

*   To run a query from the **Database** window, double click on the query name, or select the query and click **Open**.

*   To display the **Select Query** window for a query, select the query and click **Design**.

## 7.12  Calculations

There may be times when you need to carry out calculations on the data held in your tables. Calculations cannot be performed within a table, but they can be performed in a query. Let's say you wanted to calculate how much money had been spent on each title in your library.

In the *Book* table we have recorded the price of each book and also the number of copies we have in the library. To find out how much we have spent on each title we would need to multiply the value in the *Price* field by the value in the *Number of copies* field.

Rules for calculated fields in queries:

- Calculated field names must be followed by a : (colon), then by the expression to perform the calculation.

- Field names must be enclosed within square brackets [ ].

- Operators used to perform calculations are + (add), – (subtract), * (multiply), / (divide).

- Formulas must be enclosed within parentheses ( ).

To enter a formula to calculate the amount spent on each title:

1 Add the fields required to the **Query Design** grid – I have added *Category*, *Title*, *Price* and *Number of copies*.

2 In the next column in the query grid, add a field name for the calculated field – just type it in (in this example I have typed in *Value*) – followed by a colon :

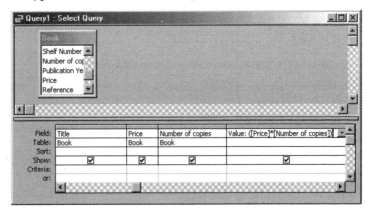

3 In the same cell, enter the formula to calculate the value, e.g. ([Price]*[No of copies])

4 Run the query and check that your calculations are correct.

- Save this query (you can simply call it *Value*) so that you can use it in the report in section 8.4 in the next chapter.

| Category | Title | Price | Number of copies | Value |
|----------|-------|-------|------------------|-------|
| Children's Fiction | In & Out Stories | £3.99 | 3 | £11.97 |
| Children's Fiction | Castaways | £4.50 | 2 | £9.00 |
| History | The 2nd World War | £12.50 | 3 | £37.50 |
| Computing | Teach Yourself Access 2002 | £8.99 | 2 | £17.98 |
| Cooking | Campfire Cooking | £4.99 | 1 | £4.99 |
| Gardening | Garden Shrubs | £4.99 | 2 | £9.98 |
| Adult Fiction | African Drums | £12.50 | 1 | £12.50 |
| Computing | Bits & Bytes | £9.99 | 2 | £19.98 |
| Travel | West Highland Way | £12.50 | 1 | £12.50 |
| Animals | Hamsters at Home | £4.50 | 1 | £4.50 |
| Travel | Giant World Atlas | £35.00 | 1 | £35.00 |
| Computing | Easy Internet | £9.99 | 2 | £19.98 |
| Astronomy | The Night Sky | £35.00 | 2 | £70.00 |
| Cooking | Bread and Biscuits | £12.50 | 2 | £25.00 |
| Astronomy | Crazy Comets | £17.50 | 1 | £17.50 |

Record: 14 ◄ 15 ► ►I ►* of 20

You can also perform a different type of calculation in a query. These are called *aggregate* functions, e.g. sum, avg, min, max and count. An aggregate function produces summary information from your data.

You could use this type of function to work out how many books you had in your library. You must add another row to the **Query Design** grid for this function – the **Totals** row.

1  To display this row, click the **Totals** tool 🗵 on the Query Design toolbar.

2  To calculate the total number of books in your library, add the *Number of copies* field to the **Query Design** grid then choose **SUM** from the options in the **Total** row.

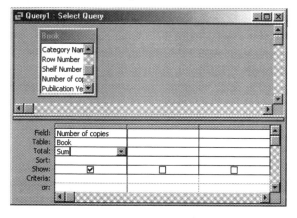

3  Run the query to find out the answer.

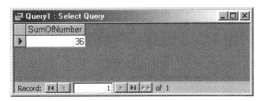

You could use a similar query to find out how many books you had in each category. Add the *Category* field to the **Query Design** grid, and choose **Group By** in the **Total** row for this field. If you want the results sorted, e.g. in ascending number of copies, set the sort order.

♦ Run the query and check the results.

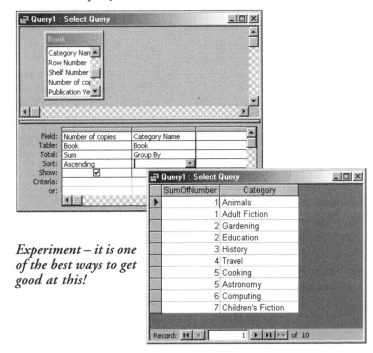

*Experiment – it is one of the best ways to get good at this!*

## Date() function and calculation

The Date() function returns the current date from your computer system as a number. Date calculations are done in *days*. You must therefore convert the days to weeks (/7) or years (/365) as required.

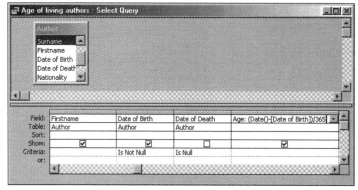

In the *Library* database the Date function could be used in a query to calculate the age of the authors. In other situations it could be used to calculate the length of service of an employee, or the length of time an item has been in stock.

In this example the **Is Null** and **Is Not Null** criteria are used to select the authors that are still alive, then the Date function is used in the calculation.

The result will display with several decimal places unless you format the *Age* field to **Fixed**, with 0 decimal places.

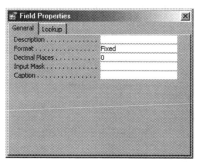

To format the *Age* field, click the **Properties** tool when the insertion point is in the field and set the properties in the dialog box.

# 7.13 Is Null/Is Not Null

You can use a query to help you locate records that have an empty field (or don't have an empty field). For example, you could use a query to display all the Publisher records that you don't have an e-mail address for.

+ To check for an empty field, you use the criteria **Is Null**.

+ To check that a field is not empty, use the criteria **Is Not Null**.

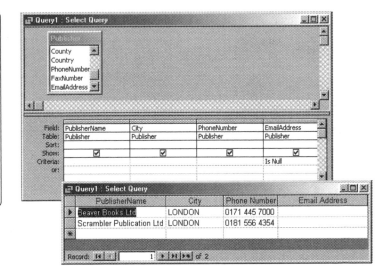

## Summary

In this chapter you have learnt how to sort the data in your tables, extract records that meet specific criteria and perform calculations.

You have learnt how to:

◆ Perform a simple sort.

◆ Perform a multi-level sort.

◆ Find records.

◆ Filter data by selection.

◆ Filter data by form.

◆ Extract data from several tables.

◆ Enter expressions into Select Queries.

◆ Set up Parameter Queries.

◆ Perform calculations on your data.

◆ Check for the presence or absence of data.

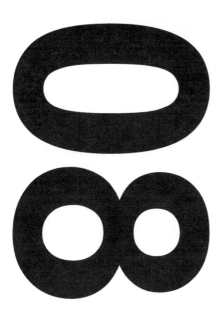

08

reports

**In this unit you will learn**

- how to create reports
- about grouping records in reports
- how to add page numbers and the date to reports
- about report calculations
- about formatting in reports
- how to create labels

## Aims of this chapter

Reports provide an effective way of producing a printed copy of the data extracted or calculated from your tables and queries.

In this chapter you will be introduced to some of the methods you can use to generate reports. You will learn how to produce reports using AutoReport, by manually designing a report and by using a Report Wizard to generate labels.

# 8.1 AutoReport

You can quickly design a simple report from any of your tables or queries using AutoReport. It will be a simple, single column report, listing all the fields in each record of the table or query.

You can create an AutoReport from an open table or query, or from the **Database** window.

**To create an AutoReport from an open table or query:**

1 Display the **New Object** list.

2 Select **AutoReport**.

A simple report will be created using the data in the open table or query.

3 When you close the report you will be asked if you want to save it. If you do, it will be shown in the **Reports** list in the **Database** window.

This report was based on the *Title, Author and Publisher details* query set up in Chapter 7.

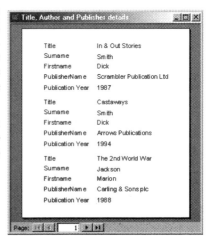

You do not need to open a table or query before you can generate an AutoReport from it – you can do so from the **Database** window.

**To generate an AutoReport from the Database window:**

1  Select the table or query you want to base your report on (*Title, Author and Publisher details* query in this example).

2  Choose **AutoReport** from the **New Object** list.

Reports are displayed in Print Preview – so you can see what your page would look like if you were to print it out.

You can use the navigation buttons at the bottom of the Print Preview window to move through the pages in your report.

On this report, the detail from several records fits on each page – the number will obviously vary from report to report as the amount of detail in some tables and queries will be considerably more than in others.

3  Click the **View** tool on the Print Preview toolbar to take your report through into Design view.

The Design view of a report looks very similar to the Design view of a form – many of the design features discussed in Chapter 6 on Forms Design are also used in report design.

The main areas in a report are the:

• **Detail** area

• **Page Header and Footer** area

• **Report Header and Footer** area.

The Page Header and Footer areas are displayed by default in an AutoReport design, and you can enter anything you want to appear at the top or bottom of each page of your report in these areas.

The Field List, containing the field names from the table or query on which the report is based, is displayed – you can toggle the display of this by clicking the **Field List** tool ▣.

# 8.2 Page Header and Footer

Page Headers are often used for column headings, or the report title; Page Footers are usually used for page numbering.

## Adding a Page Header

You can easily add a Page Header using the **Label** tool. You used the **Label** tool in Form design to add headings, instructions and other text to your form. The same techniques are used in Report design.

1  Click the **Label** tool ![label tool icon] on the toolbar.

2  Move the mouse pointer into the **Page Header** area – the mouse pointer becomes an ⁺A shape.

3  Click and drag to draw a rectangle to set the position of the text.

4  When you let go the mouse, the insertion point is within the area you have outlined.

5  Type in your header text – '*Books held in the library*'.

6  Click outside your heading when you have finished.

**To format the heading:**

7  Select the label (click on it once).

8  Use the tools on the formatting toolbar to increase the font size, change its colour, make it bold, etc.

## Adding a Page Footer

In the page footer area of a report, the page number is usually shown. The page number is placed in a *Text Box*.

1  If necessary, scroll down through your report until you see the **Page Footer** area.

2  Click the **Text Box** tool ![text box tool icon] then click and drag in the **Page Footer** area to indicate the position of the Text Box.

A **Text Box** field consists of a description (the left part) and a detail area (the right part).

3  Delete the description part – select it and press [**Delete**].

**To get Access to put a page number in the Text Box:**

4  Select the box – click on it once.

5 Type '= *[Page]*'.

6 Format the Text Box as you wish.

Your design screen should be similar to the one shown below.

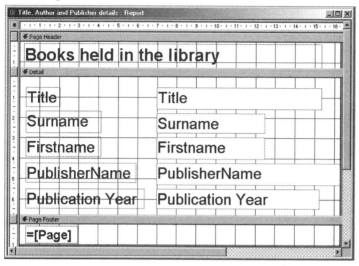

## 8.3 Save, print preview and print

1 Click the **Save** tool 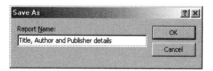 on the Report Design toolbar to save your report.

2 At the **Save As** dialog box, give your report a suitable name.

3 Click **OK**.

4 Take your form through into Print Preview to see how it looks now – note the Page Header and Footer that you have set up on each page.

5 To print your report out, click the **Print** tool on the Print Preview toolbar.

6 Close your Report to return to the **Database** window – click X on the right of the **Print Preview** title bar.

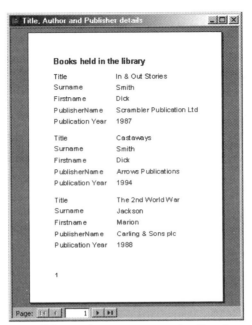

Your report will be under Reports on the Database window.

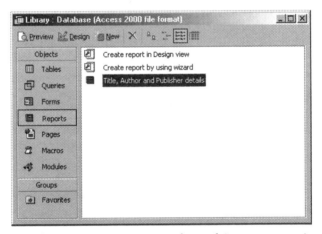

Once you have set a report up and saved it, you can print it from the **Database** window without previewing it. Select the report from the **Reports** list and click the **Print** tool on the Database toolbar.

# 8.4 Report design

You can design your own report layout, arranging the fields as you want them to appear on the design grid.

In this example, we will design a report that will display details of all the books in each category in the library – **grouped** by category. The **group header** will contain the category name, e.g. *Adult Fiction*, *Travel*, etc. In the detail area we will display:

* the title
* the number of copies held
* the price and
* the value (calculated in the *Value* query in 7.12)

for each book.

We will also display the total value of the books in each category (in a Text box in the *group footer* – see section 8.7) and the grand total for all the books in the library (in a Text box in the *report footer*– see section 8.8).

1 Select **Reports** on the Objects bar in the **Database** window and click ⬛ New .

2 At the **New Report** dialog box, select **Design View** and choose the table or query from which the data will come (in this example we will use the *Value* query).

3 Click **OK**.

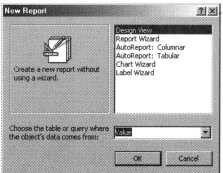

4 At the design grid, set up the **Detail** area to display the *Title*, *Number of Copies*, *Price* and *Value* data.

5 Drag the required fields from the **Field List** into the **Detail** area.

6 Delete the description part of each field (we will add column headings later) and line up the data in the **Detail** area – I suggest in a single row across the grid.

7 Decrease the size of the **Detail** area so that it will produce a neat list – drag the bottom border of the **Detail** area up – until it looks similar to the illustration below.

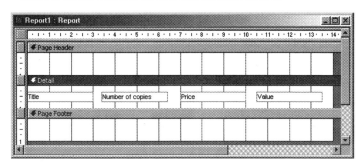

## 8.5 Layout Preview

As you are designing your report, you can preview it whenever you want to check how things are going.

If you are working with a table or query that has a lot of data in it, doing a Print Preview each time you want to check things may prove time consuming as Access prepares a preview of *all* data in your table or query. To speed things up, choose **Layout Preview** from the **View** options. Access will prepare a few pages of data – enough to check the layout.

If you want, you can do Print Preview before you send your report to the printer, to check that every page is as it should be.

## 8.6 Grouping

On this report, we want to group the books so that all the books in each Category are listed together.

This is set up in the **Sorting and Grouping** dialog box.

1 Click the **Sorting and Grouping** tool ⊞ on the Report Design toolbar to open the dialog box.

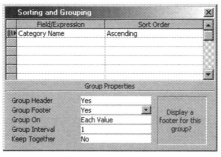

2   Select *CategoryName* from the **Field/Expression** drop-down list.

3   Set the **Sort Order** to *Ascending* – so the category groups will be in alphabetical order.

4   In the **Group Properties** pane set the **Group Header** and **Group Footer** property to *Yes* – we want a header at the beginning of each group to display the category name and a footer for one of our calculations.

5   Close the dialog box to return to your design grid.

6   Drag the *CategoryName* field from the **Field List** into the **Category Name Header** area on your grid.

7   Format it as required – as it is a heading, you might want to format it with a larger font, or bold, or both.

8   Use the **Label** tool to put column headings inside the **Category Name Header** area – these could be *Title, Number of Copies, Price* and *Value.* Format them as required.

Your report design should now be similar to this illustration.

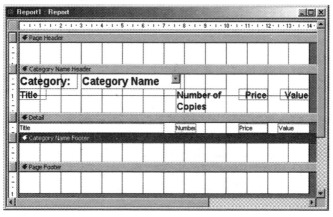

9  In the **Page Header** area, insert an appropriate heading for each page – '*Current Book Stock*'.

10 Number the pages in the **Page Footer** area – insert a Text Box, and delete the description (left) part.

If you want the footer to say *Page 1*, *Page 2*, etc. rather than simply *1, 2*, you need to enter '=*"Page "* & *[Page]*' in the Text Box.

# 8.7 Calculations

To calculate the total value of books in each category, we must add up all the values in our calculated column. This is done by adding a Text Box to the *Group Footer*, i.e. the *Category Name* footer, area to hold the formula required.

1  Add a Text Box to the *Group Footer* area.

2  Replace the text, e.g. '*Text12*', in the left bit with something like '*Value of stock in category*'.

3  In the right-hand section of the Text Box enter the formula '=*Sum([Value])*'.

This formula will add together all the amounts in the *Value* field to give the total amount for the group.

**To format the field to display the value as currency:**

1  Select the field that the total will appear in (if necessary).

2  Click 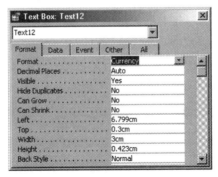 to display the Text Box properties.

3  Set the **Format** field to *Currency*.

4  Close the **Properties** dialog box.

- Remember to check out the layout of your report by going into Layout Preview or Print Preview regularly.

**Note**

Other formulas that work on the same principle include:

**Max**   to return the maximum value from a set of data, e.g. =**Max**([*fieldname*])

**Min**   to give the minimum value from a set of data, e.g. =**Min**([*fieldname*])

**Avg**   to calculate the average value for a set of data, e.g. =**Avg**([*fieldname*])

**Count**  to give the number of entries in a set of data, e.g. =**Count**([*fieldname*])

# 8.8   Report Header and Footer

A Report Header goes at the beginning of your report (at the top of the first page), a Report Footer goes at its end (at the end of the last page).

The Header is often used to describe the contents of the report; the Footer to identify the author and the date of printing.

1  To add a Report Header and Footer section, choose **Report Header/Footer** from the **View** menu.

2  In the **Report Header** area, use the **Label** tool to insert a field for your report header. Key in your header – '*Books Grouped by Category*' – and format it as required.

3  In the **Report Footer** area, insert a **Label** field and enter your name.

We also want to insert the date in the report footer.

4  Insert a Text Box and delete the description (left) part.

5  Select the **Detail** (right) part and enter '= *Date()*' – this will produce the current date in the format 19/12/2002.

You can perform summary calculations for the whole report in the *report footer*. Add a Text Box to the report footer to calculate the total value of stock. The method is the same as for calculations in a group footer (see section 8.7).

1 Add a Text Box to the *Report Footer* area.

2 Replace the text, e.g. '*Text12*', in the left bit with something like '*Total value of stock*'.

3 In the right-hand section of the Text Box enter the formula '*=Sum([Value])*'.

**To format the field to display the value as currency:**

4 Select the field that the total will appear in (if necessary).

5 Click ⊞ to display the Text Box properties.

6 Set the **Format** field to *Currency*.

7 Close the **Properties** dialog box.

# 8.9 Finishing touches

By using the Toolbox and the Formatting toolbar, you can add the finishing touches to the objects in your report (or form) by adding lines, borders, colour and special effects.

We could add a border to the *Publisher Group* heading and format the border using the options available.

**To add a border:**

1 Click the **Rectangle** tool ⊡ on the Toolbox.

2 Click and drag over the *Category Header* area – to draw a border around the label and detail parts.

When you release the mouse button, the label and detail area are hidden. This is because they are under the new rectangle. You must send this behind the text you want to show.

3 Select the rectangle if you have deselected it.

4 Open the **Format** menu and choose **Send to Back**.

The rectangle is sent behind the label and detail area and your label and detail area should be visible.

If you want a top and bottom border only, use the **Line** tool ▨. Click and drag to draw your lines wherever you want them.

You can change the line colour, thickness and add other effects.

5 Select the rectangle and experiment with the following tools to create different effects:

* Change the border colour using the **Line/Border Color** tool .

* Make the border thicker or thinner using the **Line/Border Width** tool .

* Select a different background colour using the **Fill/Back Color** tool .

* Create a special effect using the **Special Effect** tool .

Use the **Line** tool to draw a line above and below the report heading. Experiment with its formatting.

6 Save your report under *Books grouped by Category*.

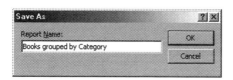

7 Preview your report and print it if you wish (see the example screenshots on the next page)

8 Close your report when you've finished – it will be listed under **Reports** in the **Database** window.

# 8.10 Labels

If any of your tables contain names and addresses, you will most probably need to prepare labels from them from time to time. Labels are very easily prepared in Access using the Label Wizard.

In this example, we will go through the steps required to produce labels for the publishers in our *Publisher* table.

1 Select **Reports** on the Objects bar in the **Database** window, and click **New** .

2 At the **New Report** dialog box, choose **Label Wizard** and select *Publisher* as the table on which to base the report. Click **OK**.

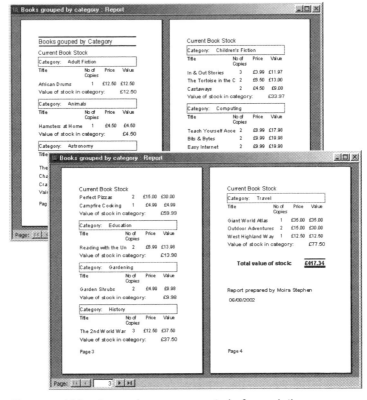

It's a good idea to preview your reports before printing.

There are lots of different label specifications for various manufacturers set up in the wizard ready for you to use (or you can click the **Customize** button to set up your own label specification).

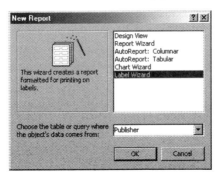

3 Select the label size required and click **Next**. Select the font and font attributes you wish to use and click **Next**.

4 Select the fields required for your label from the **Available fields** list and add them to the **Prototype label** layout.

5 Press [**Enter**] each time a new line is needed.

• If you add a field by mistake, select it in the **Prototype label** and delete it by pressing the [**Delete**] key. Click **Next**.

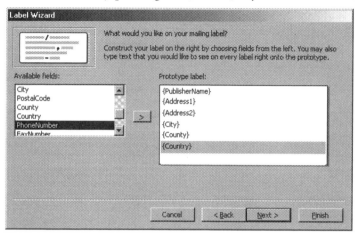

6 At the next step, specify the sort field (or fields) if required. If you want the labels printed in publisher name order, add *PublisherName* to the **Sort by** list. Click **Next**.

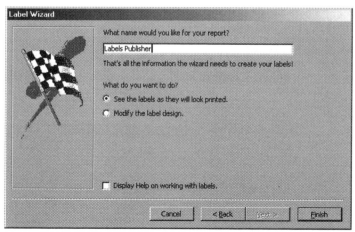

7 At the checkered flag, edit the report name if necessary (the default name is usually okay), choose **See the labels as they will look printed** and click **Finish**.

A Print Preview of the labels will appear on your screen. If you don't like the labels, you can take them into Design view and change the font or font attributes, or you could work through the wizard again specifying different criteria.

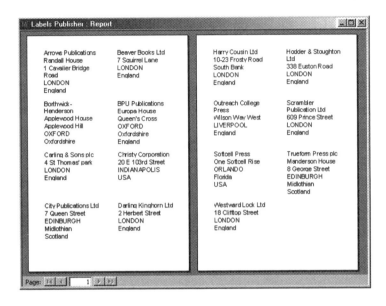

8 If you want to print your labels, load your label stationery into your printer then click the **Print** tool on the Print Preview toolbar.

When you close your report, you will find it listed in the Reports area of the Database window. If you need to print the same set of labels again, you can easily do so without having to set the whole thing up.

# Summary

In this chapter we have discussed reports, and looked at some of the ways you can use them to produce printed output from your tables and queries. You have learnt how to:

- Set up a simple report using AutoReport.

- Design a report from scratch.

- Group records within a report.

- Add page numbers to your pages.

- Print the current date on your report.

- Perform calculations in group footers and report footers.

- Add lines and borders.

- Create labels.

- Print your reports.

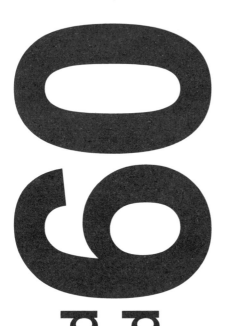

# 09 pivottables and pivotcharts

**In this unit you will learn**

- how to display data in PivotTables
- about showing/hiding and filtering data
- some calculation options
- how to display and manipulate data in a PivotChart
- about multiplots

## Aims of this chapter

This chapter will show you how to display your data using PivotTables and PivotCharts. PivotTables allow you to summarize and analyze the data and PivotCharts give a graphical representation. PivotTables and PivotCharts are dynamic and interactive – they can help you summarize and present your data very effectively.

# 9.1 PivotTable View

Open the *Book* table in Datasheet view so that you can experiment with this feature.

* Click the drop-down arrow beside the **View** tool and choose **PivotTable View**.

An empty PivotTable is displayed, with a Field List showing which fields contain the source data that you have access to.

* Click ⊟ to toggle the display of the Field List.

### The PivotTable toolbar

The PivotTable toolbar appears when you view your data as a PivotTable. Some of the tools are covered later in this chapter.

### Areas

The PivotTable contains a number of 'drop' areas – areas that you can drop the fields from your table.

### Filter

A filter field is used to confine the view to a particular part of the available data. When an item is selected in a filter field, data is displayed and calculated only for that item. If you add a Category filter field, you can have the PivotTable View display and calculate data for the categories you select.

### Row and column

Row and column fields are used to summarize and compare data. They display the unique items of data in a field either down rows or across columns. The cell at the intersection of each row and column summarizes the data for the item.

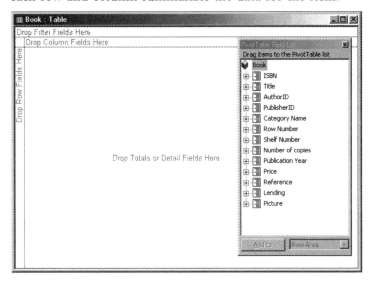

### Detail

Detail fields display the actual data – the data that is available to be summarized. They display all of the detail records from the source for these fields. Field names become column labels, with the detail records displayed in rows below them.

## Add, Remove and Move fields

You must add the fields that you wish to display in the PivotTable to the row, column, filter and detail area (you don't need to add fields to all areas).

Field names in the Field List that are **bold** have already been added to the PivotTable, those that are not bold can be added as required.

### To add a field:

• Drag and drop the field into the appropriate area (depending on how you wish to filter and analyze your data).

Or

1  Select the field you wish to add to the PivotTable.

2  Choose the area that you want to add it to from the options (at bottom of Field List).

3  Click **Add To**.

**To remove a field:**

1  Right-click on the field name in the PivotTable.

2  Left-click on **Remove**.

Add the following fields to the areas suggested:

| | |
|---|---|
| **Filter** | Category Name and Publisher ID |
| **Row** | Title |
| **Column** | Number of copies |
| **Detail** | Price |

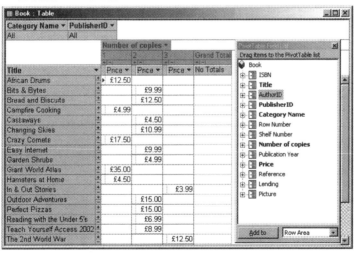

**To move a field:**

You can move fields from one area to another using drag and drop.

Watch the icon that appears at the mouse pointer as you drag and drop – it lets you know which area you are over.

Your data will 'pivot' when you move your fields – hence the name!

| Book : Table | | | | |
|---|---|---|---|---|
| **Category Name ▼** | **PublisherID ▼** | | | |
| All | All | | | |
| | | | Drop Column Fields Here | |
| **Title** ▼ | **Number of copies** ▼ | **Price** ▼ | | |
| ⊞ African Drums | 1 | ▶ £12.50 | | |
| ⊞ Bits & Bytes | 2 | £9.99 | | |
| ⊞ Bread and Biscuits | 2 | £12.50 | | |
| ⊞ Campfire Cooking | 1 | £4.99 | | |
| ⊞ Castaways | 2 | £4.50 | | |
| ⊞ Changing Skies | 2 | £10.99 | | |
| ⊞ Crazy Comets | 1 | £17.50 | | |
| ⊞ Easy Internet | 2 | £9.99 | | |
| ⊞ Garden Shrubs | 2 | £4.99 | | |
| ⊞ Giant World Atlas | 1 | £35.00 | | |
| ⊞ Hamsters at Home | 1 | £4.50 | | |
| ⊞ In & Out Stories | 3 | £3.99 | | |
| ⊞ Outdoor Adventures | 2 | £15.00 | | |
| ⊞ Perfect Pizzas | 2 | £15.00 | | |
| ⊞ Reading with the Under 5's | 2 | £6.99 | | |
| ⊞ Teach Yourself Access 2002 | 2 | £8.99 | | |
| ⊞ The 2nd World War | 3 | £12.50 | | |
| ⊞ The Night Sky | 2 | £35.00 | | |
| ⊞ The Tortoise in the Corner | 2 | £6.50 | | |

## Show/Hide buttons

If you look closely you will notice plus and minus signs at the **Row** ⬚ and **Column** ⬚⬚ areas.

These are used to show and hide the information in that row or column.

* Click the + button to show the data.
* Click the – button to hide the data.

### Show Details/Hide Details

You can also use the **Show Details/Hide Details** tools to toggle the display of your data.

**To show or hide all the data:**

1 Select the **Filter**, **Row**, **Column** or **Data** field name.

2 Click the **Show Details** ⬚ or **Hide Details** ⬚ tool.

* You can show/hide the information in individual rows and columns if you select the row or column then click the **Show Details** or **Hide Details** tool.

## Filter

Use the Filter fields to display specific sets of data.

1 Click the drop-down arrow beside the field you wish to filter on, e.g. **Category**.

2 Deselect the **All** checkbox.

3 Select the category(s) that you wish to display.

4 Click **OK**.

### AutoFilter

Click the **AutoFilter** tool to toggle between showing all the items in your PivotTable and those specified in a Filtered list.

## Show Top/Bottom items

You can choose to show the top or bottom items in your rows or columns.

1 Click on the row heading or column heading area.

2 Click the **Show Top/Bottom** items tool.

3 Select **Show Only the Top** or **Show Only the Bottom**.

4 Click on the number of items required.

## AutoCalc and Subtotal

Calculations can be performed on the data identified in the rows and column.

**To add a Subtotal row or column:**

1 Select the row or column field name.

2 Click the **Subtotal** tool .

## To perform an automatic calculation:

1 Select the row or column field name.
2 Click the **AutoCalc** tool.
3 Select the type of calculation required from the list.

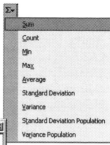

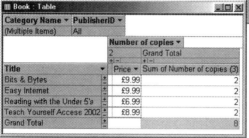

When you have performed calculations on your data, an entry appears under **Totals** in the Field List.

If you perform several calculations on your data, there will be multiple entries under **Totals**.

You can remove your calculations from the PivotTable in the normal way (right-click on the column heading, then click on **Remove**).

The calculation is not deleted – it remains in the Field List and can be added to the PivotTable again (double-click on it).

* To delete a calculation, right-click on it in the Field List and click **Delete**.

## Collapse/Expand

If you have more than one field in the row or column area, you can use the **Collapse** and **Expand** tools to control the number of rows and columns displayed.

### To collapse or expand the detail:

1 Select the row or column heading.

2  Click the **Collapse** 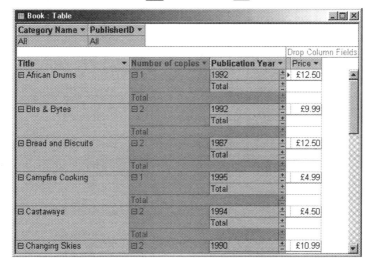 or **Expand**  tool.

## 9.2 PivotCharts

A PivotChart gives a graphical representation of your data.

**To go into PivotChart View:**

1  Open your table.

2  Select **PivotChart View** from the **View** options.

If you have a PivotTable set up, the data in it will be displayed in **PivotChart View**.  If you have no PivotTable set up an empty chart layout is displayed.

The PivotChart toolbar is also displayed.

Working in a PivotChart is very similar to working in a PivotTable.  You can add, remove and move the fields to display the data as required.

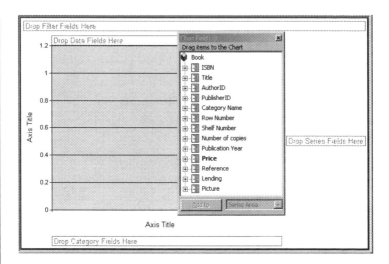

## Add, remove and move fields

You must add the fields that you wish to display in the PivotChart to the filter, category, series and data areas (you don't need to add fields to all areas).

**To add a field:**

* Drag and drop the field into the appropriate area (depending on how you wish to filter and analyze your data).

Or

1 Select the field you wish to add to the PivotChart.

2 Choose the area that you want to add it to from the options (at bottom of Field List).

3 Click **Add To**.

**To remove a field:**

1 Click on the field in the PivotChart.

2 Click the **Delete** tool ⊠ on the toolbar.

Add the following fields to the areas suggested:

| | |
|---|---|
| **Filter** | Publisher ID |
| **Series** | Category |
| **Data** | Number of copies |

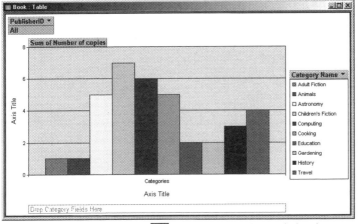

- Click the **Legend** tool to toggle the legend display.
- Click the drop-down arrows beside the filter and legend fields to control the amount of data displayed.

**To move a field:**

- Drag and drop the fields from one area to another to move them and 'pivot' the data.

## Edit the chart type

1 Click the **Chart Type** tool to display the **Properties** dialog box.

2 Select the **Type** tab.

3 Pick a type from the list of charts down the left.

4 Choose a chart from the options displayed on the right.

5 Close the **Properties** dialog box.

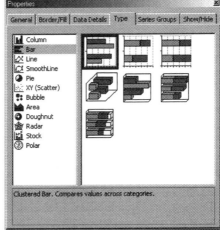

## By row/By column

Click the 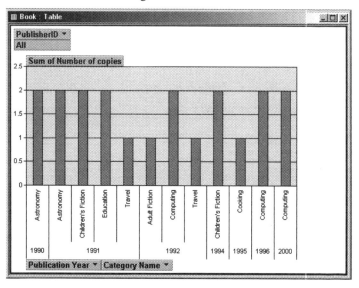 to swap the change from a by-row representation of the data to a by-column one.

## Multiple series

You can plot more than one series of data on your chart. In this example both *Publication Year* and *Category Name* have been added to the Category fields area.

*Publication Year* is at the **outer** level, and *Category Name* is at an **inner** level. The effect this has is that it plots the data in the outer level, and then moves to the right plotting the inner levels within the higher level.

## Multiple Plots/Unified Scale

You can display separate graphs on the same PivotChart to view your data, e.g. a separate graph for each sales person in your team. This feature is useful when you want to compare different sets of data.

**To create multiple plots:**

1 Click the **Multiple Plots** tool ▦ on the toolbar.

2 Drop the field that you want to create your multiple plots from into the **MultiChart Field** area.

A separate chart will be produced for each item.

To make it easier to compare the data in the charts, if may be useful to display them all using the same scale.

• Click the **MultiPlots Unified Scale** tool ▦ to unify the scale across the charts.

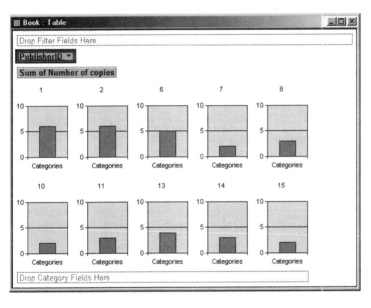

# Summary

In this chapter we have looked at PivotTables and PivotCharts. We have:

* Displayed data in a PivotTable.

* Added, removed and moved fields in a PivotTable.

* Used Show and Hide options.

* Filtered the data.

* Performed automatic calculations.

* Displayed data in a PivotChart.

* Added, removed and moved fields in a PivotChart.

* Toggled the Legend display.

* Selected a different Chart Type.

* Arranged data by row and by column.

* Specified multiple series.

* Discussed Multiple Plots and MultiPlots Unified Scale.

# 10

## data access pages

**In this unit you will learn**

- how to create and use a data access page
- some options for the page heading
- how to add a theme
- how to open at a blank page
- how to find out about publishing your page

## Aims of this chapter

This chapter discusses data access pages. If you wish to view and work on data from an Access database on an intranet or the Internet you can do so using a data access page. You can also use a data access page as an alternative to a form. There are three main uses for data access pages: data entry (for viewing, adding and editing records), interactive reporting (to publish summaries of data held in a database) and data analysis. We will discuss the first of these – data entry.

# 10.1 Creating a page using a wizard

The easiest way to create your page is by using the wizard.

In this example we create a data access page that allows the public to view the stock we hold in our library. The stock will be grouped by category, and the list of books sorted into order on author name.

**To create a data access page using the wizard:**

1 Select **Pages** in the Objects list in the **Database** window and click **New** 📇New .

2 Select **Page Wizard** from the **New Data Access Page** dialog box.

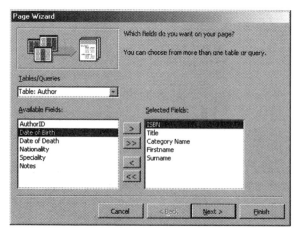

3 Choose the table or query from which the data comes – *Book* in this example – and click **OK**.

4 Add the fields required from the table to the **Selected Fields:** list – *ISBN*, *Title* and *Category Name*.

5 If you want fields from a different table or query, select it from the **Tables/Queries** drop-down list.

6 Add the fields required from each table/query until you have the set of fields you require, e.g *Firstname* and *Surname* from the *Author* table – and click **Next**.

7 Add a **Grouping Level** if necessary – we will group by *Category Name*. Click **Next**.

8 Set the sort order, e.g. by *Surname* then *Firstname*. Click **Next**.

9 At the checkered flag, enter a title for your page (or accept the one suggested), choose **Open the Page** and click **Finish**.

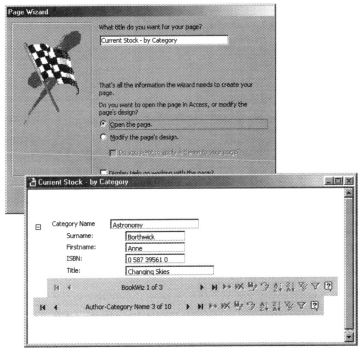

The page has an **Expand/Collapse** button beside the category name. The navigation bars let you move through the books or the categories.

The page is *read only*. You cannot add, edit or delete records. When you specify a grouping option on a data access page the page will be read only. As you would not want the general public to be able to amend these pages, read only status is perfect.

Take the data access page into Design view to see how it is set up. The design grid is similar to that of forms and reports, with a number of different options specifically for data access pages.

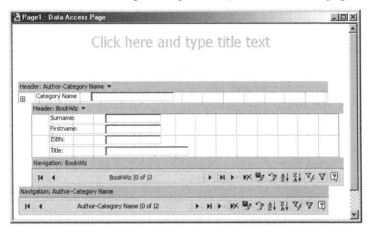

## 10.2 Close and save

Save your data access page.

1 Click the **Save** tool on the Page Design toolbar.

2 Choose the folder it will be saved in.

3 Give it a name.

4 Click **Save**.

If you close your data access page without saving it, you will be prompted to do so. Click **Yes** at the prompt to save your page.

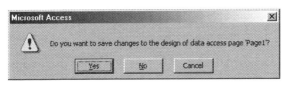

A shortcut to the data access page will be listed under **Pages** on the **Database** window.

---

**Note**

The data access page is not stored within your database file. It is stored at the location indicated in the **Save As** dialog box. The object listed in the database window is a shortcut to the page.

---

# 10.3 Creating a page in Design view

If you are using a database in a library situation, an obvious use for the database is to record and maintain details of the members of the library. This example is based on a *Members* table (which you can quickly set up using either Table wizard or Table Design view). The table structure would be something like the one in the screenshot on the next page:

• You must set up your table, specify the primary key and save the table before you can create a data access page for it.

We will create a data access page that will allow details of new members to be added – either on the library intranet or over the Internet. This will allow new members to add their own details to the membership table directly (rather than by filling in a paper form).

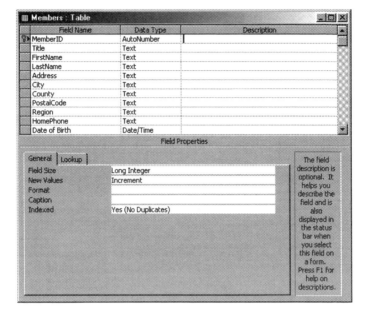

1 Select **Pages** on the Objects list in the **Database** window.

2 Click 🔲 New .

3 Select **Design View** from the **New Data Access Page** dialog box.

4 Choose the table or query from which the data comes – *Members* in this example.

5 Click **OK**.

You will arrive in data access page Design view, with the Field List displayed. Click 🔳 to toggle the display of the Field List if necessary.

### Field List

The Field List is similar to that displayed in Forms or Reports design. The main difference is that all the tables/queries in the database are displayed – either in the *Tables* folder, or the *Queries* folder. You can use the scrollbars to bring the folders into view if necessary. Simply double-click on a folder, or on a table or query, to toggle the display of its contents.

## To add a field to the data access page:

1 Drag the fields from the Field List and drop them on the page.

Or

2 Select the field name in the list.

3 Click 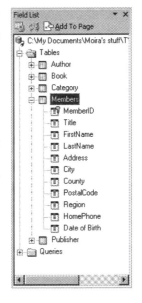 .

* The fields are added to the Header section of the data access page.

Move or resize fields in the same way as in Forms or Reports design.

## To move a field:

1 Select it.

2 Drag the field to its new location.

## To resize a field:

1 Select it.

2 Drag one of the selection handles until it the required size.

## Navigation Bar

At the end of your data access page is the *NavigationSection*. This section contains the buttons required to move through your pages, add, delete, save, sort, filter, etc.

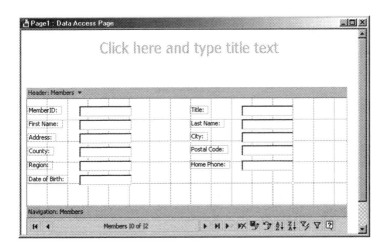

## Page Heading

At the top of the data access page is an area for your page heading. You could just follow the prompt – *Click here and type title text* – or you could insert a scrolling text object to have your heading scroll across the screen.

## Scrolling text

Scrolling text can be effective for a page heading, or for instructions to the user of the page. Don't scroll all the text in headings and instructions – the page will look too confusing!

1 Click the **Scrolling Text** tool ▣ on the Toolbox.

2 Drag over the area that you want the scrolling text to appear – an object containing *Marquee()* will appear.

3 Replace the *Marquee()* prompt with the text you want.

4 Click outside the object.

## Themes

You can format your data access page using any of the formatting options available on the Formatting (Page) toolbar, or you could add a 'theme' to your page.

**To add a theme:**

1 Open the **Format** menu.

2 Choose **Theme...**

3 Select the theme you wish to use from the list.

4 Click **OK**.

## Opening to a blank page

In the example we are using (a data access page that allows new member details to be added), we would want to prevent members of the public viewing the personal details of other members in our library. It is therefore important that we set up the data access page so that a new blank page should be displayed, ready for data input, when the page is opened.

**To open to a blank page:**

1 Select the whole page – choose **Select Page** from the **Edit** menu.

2 At the **Properties** dialog box, set the **DataEntry** field (on the **Data** tab) to *True*.

3 Close the **Page properties** dialog box.

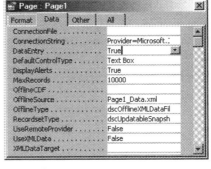

With the DataEntry property set to *True*, it is not possible to scroll through the details that have been added on earlier occasions.

• Remember to save your data access page. You don't have to wait until you have completed it – save it regularly.

Take your page into Page view to check the layout. You can jump between Design and Page view as often as you wish when setting up your page.

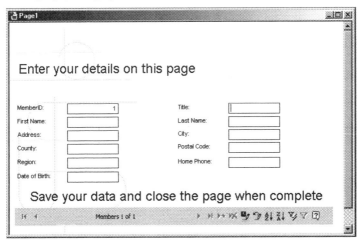

### Check it out

You should of course check that your page works correctly.

1 Go into Page view.

2 Press [**Tab**] to move from field to field.

3 Complete the fields.

4 Click the **Save** tool ![icon] on the navigation bar to save the record.

Close ⊠ the data access page and open the table that it is based on (*Members*). You should find your new record listed.

• Any time that you open the page, you should be presented with a blank page ready for data entry.

To display the page as it will appear on your intranet or the Internet, open the **File** menu and choose **Web Page Preview** (you can do this from Design view or Page view).

# 10.4  Publishing your page

Once your data access pages have been set up, you can use them in Access (as an alternative to forms) or you can publish them to your intranet or the Internet. If you are going to publish, you should contact your system administrator or Internet Service Provider (ISP) to find out how to do this in your particular case. To transfer your pages you will probably use either Web folders or File Transfer Protocol.

For additional information look on the **Contents** tab in the online help – *Using Office Programs with Web Sites, Working with Network Places and Publishing your Office Files as Web Pages.*

---

### Summary

In this chapter we have discussed data access pages. You have learnt how to:

• Create a data access page using a wizard and Design view.

• Add fields from the Field list.

• Move and resize fields.

• Add a page heading in normal or scrolling text.

• Add a theme to your page.

• Open to a blank page.

• Display a Web Page Preview.

• Find out about publishing to your intranet or the Internet.

---

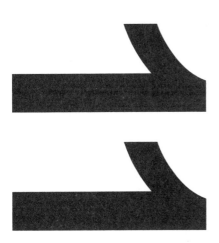

# 11

# database
# wizard

**In this unit you will learn**

- how to create a database using a wizard
- how switchboards make using a database easy
- how to display the database window behind the switchboards

## Aims of this chapter

In this chapter we will look at a quick and easy alternative to setting up our database from scratch. Here we will use a wizard to automate the process of setting up our database, rather than use the Blank database as we did in the Library example.

You should close the Library database if it is open.

# 11.1 Database Wizards

Access comes complete with several database wizards that automate the process of setting up a database. The wizards include things like Order Entry, Event Management and Expenses – they are quite varied and worth looking at, as they may save you a lot of setting up time.

1  Click the **New** tool 🗋 on the Database toolbar.

2  At the **New File** Task Pane, select **General Templates** from the **New From Template** list.

3  Select the **Database** tab.

4  Select the wizard you want to use – in this case **Event Management** – and click **OK**.

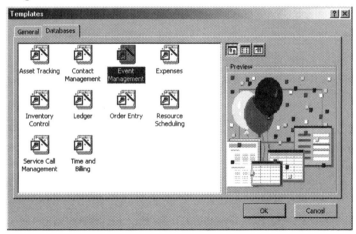

**5** Give your database a suitable name – *Course lists* in my case – and click **Create**.

The first wizard screen will give you a list of what will be stored in the database, in this case:

- Event information
- Event attendee information
- Event registration information
- Event type information
- Information about employees
- Event pricing information.

**6** Click **Next** to move onto the next step.

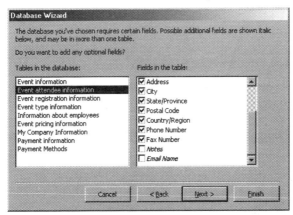

You are presented with the list of tables that will be included in your database down the left-hand side of the dialog box.

If you select a table on the left side, a list of the fields that will be set up in that table is displayed down the right side.

If you look through the list of fields for any table, you will find most of the field names have a tick beside them – they are selected for inclusion in the table. Optional fields are displayed in italics.

**7** Look through the tables and select any optional fields as required. Click **Next**.

**8** At the next step, choose a style for the screen displays in your database. Click **Next**.

9  Select the style you want to use for the reports you will be printing. Click **Next**.

10 At the next step, enter your database title, e.g. *Course Management*. If you want a picture on your reports, select the **Yes, I'd like to include a picture** checkbox, then click the **Picture...** button and choose one to include (you will find lots in the *ClipArt* folder in the *Program Files MS Office* folder to choose from). Click **Next**.

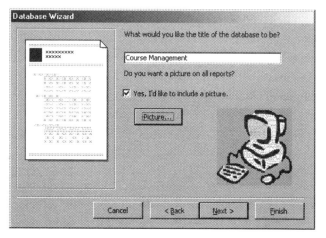

11 At the checkered flag, if you want help on using the database, select the **Display Help on using a database** checkbox. (If you have worked through the book this far, you should not need to display any help!)  Click **Finish**.

Access will spend a little time building your database. Depending on the database selected, you may be asked to provide information about your organization.

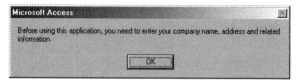

1  Click **OK**.

2  Complete the form displayed with information required.

3  Click the **Close** button at the top right of the form when you have completed it.

| My Company Information | | | |
|---|---|---|---|
| Enter your company's name and address information here. You will save the information by closing the form. | | | |
| Company Name | Stephen Associates | Sales Tax Rate | 0.00% |
| Address | 12 High Street | Payment Terms | |
| City | EDINBURGH | Invoice Descr | |
| State/Province | Midlothian | | |
| Postal Code | EH10 4ZZ | | |
| Country/Region | Scotland | | |
| Phone Number | | | |
| Fax Number | | | |

# 11.2 Exploring your database

The database will be open on your screen, ready for use. The **Database** window for your database is minimized (you can see it at the bottom left of your screen).

The **Main Switchboard** for your database is displayed. This is an alternative to the **Database** window and is perhaps more user friendly. You use the Switchboard to navigate through your forms and reports, and to enter and update data in the tables.

* If you choose a different wizard at 10.1, the forms, etc. will be different from those illustrated, but the principles are the same.

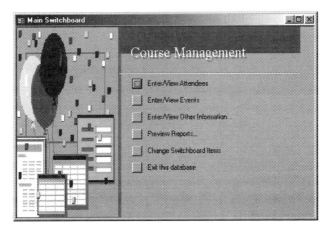

| Main Switchboard | |
|---|---|
| **Course Management** | |
| | Enter/View Attendees |
| | Enter/View Events |
| | Enter/View Other Information... |
| | Preview Reports... |
| | Change Switchboard Items |
| | Exit this database |

# 11.3 Enter/View Attendees

This option displays the *Attendees* form. It is made up of text boxes, subforms and so on, which we discussed when setting up the *Library* forms in Chapter 6.

You can add new attendees, delete existing attendees or edit the detail on any attendee from this form.

In addition to the detail fields, there are buttons which take you through to other forms in your database.

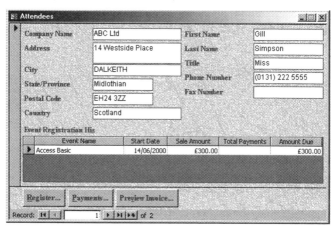

### Other forms in the Course list database

The **Register...** button takes you through to the *Registration* form.

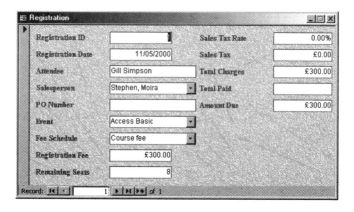

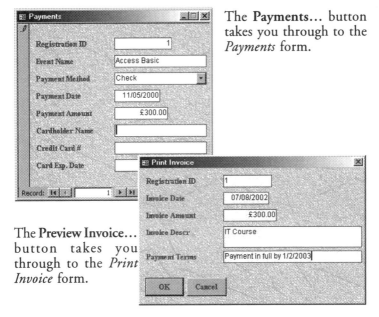

The **Payments...** button takes you through to the *Payments* form.

The **Preview Invoice...** button takes you through to the *Print Invoice* form.

Click **OK** to see a preview of the invoice.

# 11.4 Enter/View Events

This form displays a list of details for each event (course), giving names of attendees, number of places left, etc.

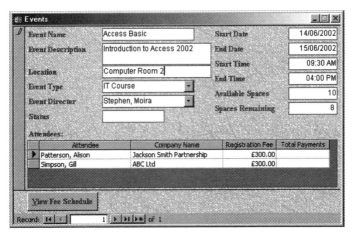

# 11.5 Enter/View Other Information

This option takes you through to the **Forms Switchboard** which lists the forms that will display the other information in your database. The forms display details on:

* Payment methods
* My company information
* Fee schedules
* Employees
* Event types.

The forms have been designed using the techniques discussed in Chapter 6. They contain text boxes, checkboxes and subforms.

You can edit the design of any of these forms by taking them into Design view.

* When you have finished exploring the forms, return to the **Main Switchboard**.

# 11.6 Preview Reports

Several reports have been set up by the wizard. These are listed in the **Reports Switchboard**. In this example we have:

* Sales by Event Type
* Sales by Employee
* Attendee Listing.

If you opted to display a picture on your reports, you will notice the picture on the reports you preview.

Some of the reports are simple lists, others have the contents grouped into categories, e.g. Sales by Employee.

Notice the **Page Header/Footer** sections in this report. The **Page Header** contains the column headings and the **Page Footer** contains the current date and page number.

* Return to the **Main Switchboard** when you have finished previewing your reports.

**Attendee Listing**

| Attendee Name | Company Name | City/State | Phone Number | Fax Number | Registrations |
|---|---|---|---|---|---|
| Patterson, Alison | Jackson Smith Partnership | Edinburgh, Midlothian | | | 1 |
| Simpson, Gill | ABC Ltd | DALKEITH, Midlothian | (0131) 222 5555 | | 1 |

*07 August 2002*                                                 *Page 1 of 1*

# 11.7  Change Switchboard Items

This option lets you edit the Switchboards that have been set up for the database. You can change the default Switchboard (the Main Switchboard in this database), add new items to Switchboards, edit existing items, and delete items from Switchboards.

We will set up our own Switchboards in Chapter 11 and work with this feature. Return to the Main Switchboard.

# 11.8  Closing the Switchboard

If you close the Main Switchboard by clicking its ⊠ **Close** button, the database remains open; you've simply closed the Switchboard 'user interface' to it. The Switchboard is a form, listed under **Forms** on the **Database** window. You can open the Switchboard again by opening the Switchboard form.

# 11.9  Exit this database

This option closes the database.

# 11.10  Database window

You may have noticed the **Database** window minimized at the bottom left of your screen.

If you restore the **Database** window, you will find the tables, queries, forms and reports listed on the tabs within the **Database** window as usual.

You can check out the design of any of the tables, queries, forms or reports and edit them if you wish.

## Warning

**Do not** edit the Switchboard form in **Form Design** View – you may find that it no longer works!

## Summary

This chapter has introduced you to the database wizards. Database wizards automate the process of setting up a database and can save you a lot of time – as long as you can find one that is useful to you! You have learnt how to:

* Create a new database using a wizard.

* Navigate your way through your database using the Switchboards.

* Explore the forms and reports within your database via a Switchboard.

* Display the Database window of the database that has been created using a wizard.

# switchboards

**In this unit you will learn**

- how to create switchboards
- about adding and editing switchboard items
- how to add a picture to your switchboard
- how to display the switchboard when the database is opened

# 12.1 Creating the Main Switchboard

You can create a Switchboard for any database you build. It is often easier to navigate through a database using a Switchboard. If you are designing a database for someone else to use, a Switchboard will distance them from the tables and design code to a considerable extent.

To create a Switchboard, the database you want to create it for must be open.

1 Open your *Library* database if it is not already open.
2 Choose **Database Utilities** from the **Tools** menu.
3 Pick **Switchboard Manager** from the list.
4 If you are prompted to create a Switchboard, click **Yes**.

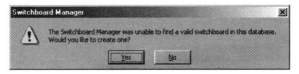

Access will create a Switchboard Items table on the Tables list in the Database window and a Switchboard form on the Forms list.

The **Switchboard Manager** dialog box will appear, with the Main Switchboard listed on it. From here, you can add items to the main Switchboard and create other Switchboards.

The first thing you need to do is decide where you want to be able to go to from the Main Switchboard. Is it to other Switchboards or directly into a form or report? In most cases it will be a mixture of both.

In this example we need to set up two more Switchboards that can be accessed from the Main Switchboard – one to list most of our forms and one for our reports.

## 12.2 Creating extra Switchboards

1 Click the **New...** button.

2 Enter a name for your Switchboard and click **OK**.

You could call the form Switchboard *Edit/View Forms* and the report Switchboard *Preview Reports*.

## 12.3 Adding to the Main Switchboard

You must now add the items you want to appear on the Main Switchboard. Here are three such items.

### Item 1

First, we want to list an option to take us to the **Edit/View Forms Switchboard** and then one to take us to the **Preview Reports Switchboard**.

1 Select the **Main Switchboard** at the **Switchboard Manager** dialog box.

2 Click the **Edit...** button.

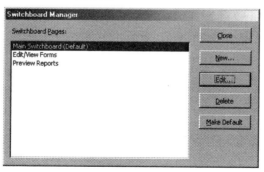

This takes you to the **Edit Switchboard Page** dialog box where you can set up the items you want on your Main Switchboard.

3  Click **New…** to add a new item to the Switchboard.

4  At the **Edit Switchboard Item** dialog box, enter the text you want to appear on the Main Switchboard page, e.g. '*Enter/View other information*'.

5  Pick the appropriate command from the command list (**Go to Switchboard** for this one).

6  Select the Switchboard you want this option to take you to in the Switchboard field, e.g. **Edit/View Forms**.

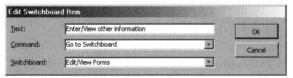

7  Click **OK**.

8  Now do the same for the **Preview Reports Switchboard**.

This time the **Text** to go on the main Switchboard could be *Preview Reports*, the **Command** would be *Go to Switchboard* and the **Switchboard** would be *Preview Reports* (if that was what you called it ).

## Item 2

We also want to add an option to the Main Switchboard to take us to the *Books, Authors and Publishers* form as we use this most often.

1  From the **Edit Switchboard** dialog box, click **New…**

2  In the **Text** field, enter the text you want to appear on the Main Switchboard, e.g. '*Book details*'.

3  In the **Command** field, choose **Open Form in Edit Mode**.

4  In the **Form** field choose *Book, Author and Publisher details*.

5  Click **OK**.

## Item 3

Finally, we need to add an option to close the database.

1 From the **Edit Switchboard Page** dialog box, click **New...**

2 In the **Text** field, enter the text you want to appear on the Main Switchboard, e.g. '*Close Database*'.

3 In the **Command** field, choose **Exit Application**.

4 Click **OK**.

You have now successfully set up the options required on your Main Switchboard.

At the **Edit Switchboard Page**, check the order of the options you have listed. The option most often used should be at the top of the list – *Book details* in our case.

1 To move *Book details* up to the top of the list, select it and click the **Move Up** button until it is in position.

2 Close the **Edit Switchboard Page** dialog box.

# 12.4 Adding to other Switchboards

This is done in the same way as setting up the Main Switchboard.

### The Edit/View Forms Switchboard

In this Switchboard, you will need to set up an option for each form you wish to view, and one to return you to the Main Switchboard.

1 Select the *Edit/View Forms* Switchboard in the **Switchboard Manager** dialog box.

2 Click **Edit...**

3 Add the required items, e.g. the forms that you have created and that are on the **Forms** tab of your *Library* database.

**To add the Publisher detail form:**

1 Click **New...** at the **Edit Switchboard Page** dialog box.

2 Enter the text you want to appear listed on your *Edit/View Forms* Switchboard, e.g. '*Publisher names and addresses*'.

3 Choose **Open Form in Edit Mode** in the **Command** field.

4 Select the *Publisher detail form* from the list of forms available in the **Form** field.

5 Click **OK**.

If you have forgotten what forms you have, and can't think of what to enter into the **Text** field, complete the **Command** and **Form** fields first, then go back to the **Text** once you know what the form is. The text does not have to be the same as the form name, etc., but you will obviously want it to reflect what will be displayed.

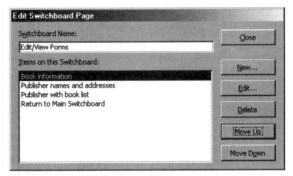

The items on your *Edit/View Forms* Switchboard should be similar to those illustrated on the previous page.

♦ Close the **Edit Switchboard Page** dialog box.

**The Preview Reports Switchboard**

In the Preview Reports Switchboard, you will need to set up an option for each report you want to preview.

You will also need to set up an option to return you to the Main Switchboard.

1 Select the *Preview Reports* Switchboard in the **Switchboard Manager** dialog box.

2 Click **Edit...**

3  Add the items required to the *Preview Reports* Switchboard.

**To add the Title, Author and Publisher report:**

1  Click **New...** at the **Edit Switchboard Page** dialog box.

2  Enter the text you want to appear listed on your *Preview Reports* Switchboard, e.g. '*Books currently held*'.

3  Choose **Open Report** in the **Command** field.

4  Select the Title, Author and Publisher details from the list of reports available in the **Report** field.

5  Click **OK**.

If you have forgotten what reports you have to choose from, and can't think of what to enter into the **Text** field, complete the **Command** field and **Report** field first, then go back to the **Text** field once you know what report you are dealing with.

Your *Preview Reports* Switchboard should be similar to the one below.

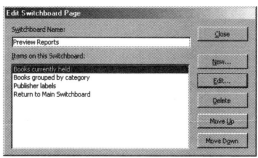

## Closing and testing

**To close Switchboard Manager:**

1  Click **Close** at the **Edit Switchboard Page** dialog box.

2  Click **Close** at the **Switchboard Manager** dialog box.

**To try your new Switchboards out:**

1  Open the **Switchboards** form on the **Forms** list in your **Database** window.

2  If the Switchboards don't work as expected go back into Switchboard Manager (select **Tools > Database Utilities > Switchboard Manager**) and check the options you set up.

# 12.5 Adding a picture

In the Switchboards created using the Database wizards, a picture is included down the left side of the Switchboard.

You can easily add a picture to your own Switchboards.

1 Close the Switchboard if necessary and return to the **Database** window.

You will find a Switchboard form displayed on your **Forms** list. To add a picture to this form you must take it into Design View. ***Do not*** edit anything else on the form.

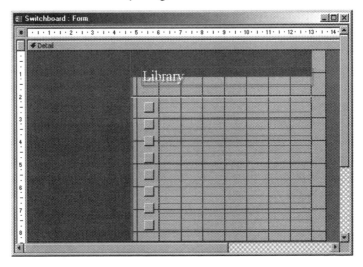

2 Select your Switchboard form and click **Design**.

3 Select the left side of the form under the **Detail** border – click in the space once.

An Image object has been set up here, ready to display the picture of your choice.

4 Click the **Properties** tool ▦ to open the **Image Properties** dialog box.

5 Select the **Format** tab or the **All** tab within the **Image Properties** dialog box.

6 Locate the **Picture** field – it is at the top of the list on the **Format** tab, or second on the list on the **All** tab.

7 Enter the path and filename of the picture you want to use.

If you do not know the path or filename, click the **Build** button 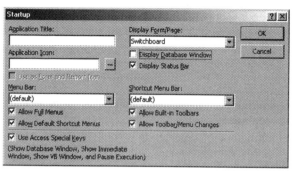 to the right of the **Picture** field and navigate through your folders until you have found the picture you want to use. There are lots of pictures in *C:\Program Files\Microsoft Office\ClipArt* to choose from.

8 Experiment with the **Size Mode** options to get the effect you want from your picture.

9 Close the **Image** dialog box when you have finished and save the changes to your form.

10 Return to **Form** view.

You should find that the picture is displayed on all of your Switchboards.

# 12.6 Starting at the Switchboard

Once you have set your Switchboard up, you will most often want to use it as the 'user interface' to your database.

You can get Access to display your Switchboard form automatically (rather than the Database window) when you open your database.

1 With the database open, choose **Startup...** from the **Tools** menu.

2 Select **Switchboard** from the list of forms available in the **Display Form** field.

3 Deselect the **Display Database Window** checkbox.

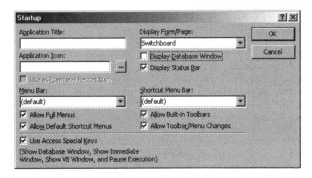

4   Click **OK**.

The next time you open your database the Main Switchboard will appear on your screen.

## Summary

In this chapter you have learnt how to set up a Switchboard for your database.

You have learnt how to:

◆ Create the Main Switchboard.

◆ Create additional Switchboards.

◆ Add items to the Switchboards.

◆ Include a picture on your Switchboard.

◆ Display the Switchboard automatically each time you open your database.

# 13

## macros and modules

### In this unit you will learn

- about creating and running macros
- how to assign a macro to a control button

## Aims of this chapter

In this chapter we will introduce macros and modules. Both are extremely powerful – this offers only a glimpse of what is possible. If you wish to become an Access 'guru', perhaps developing applications for other users, you can check out the on-line help to find out more about these objects.

# 13.1 Introducing macros

In Chapter 11 on Database Wizard we set up a *Course List* database. From the *Attendees* form, you could move to the *Registrations*, *Payments* and *Preview Invoice* forms by clicking on a button. The buttons had been placed in the **Form Footer** area in **Form Design** view. We could set up a similar routine when working in our *Library* database.

In our *Library* database, the main form that we use is the *Book, Author and Publisher* one. If you are viewing this form and discover that you need to view any other form, it can be quite tedious going back to the database window to open another, or moving and re-sizing windows to fit several on screen at once.

A more efficient option is to set up control buttons similar to those in the *Course List* database within the *Book, Author and Publisher* form, and open the other forms you need to view from within the *Book, Author and Publisher* form.

One way of achieving this is to set up a macro containing the instructions to open the required form, then assign this macro to a control button within the *Book, Author and Publisher* form.

You can use macros for many things. The list below gives only a few examples.

- ◆ Open any table, form, query or report in any available view.
- ◆ Close any open table, form, query or report.
- ◆ Open a report in Print Preview.
- ◆ Send a report to the printer.
- ◆ Execute any of the commands on the Access menus.

We will set up some very simple macros to add to our *Book, Author and Publisher* form.

# 13.2 Recording a macro

Let's say we had decided that we wanted to be able to open our *Publisher detail* form and our *Books grouped by category* report from within the *Book, Author and Publisher* form.

The first thing we need to do is record two macros:

* one containing the instructions to open the *Publisher detail* form in Form view
* one containing the instructions to open the *Books grouped by category* report in Print Preview.

## Recording a macro

* Select **Macros** in the Objects list in the **Database** window and click **New** 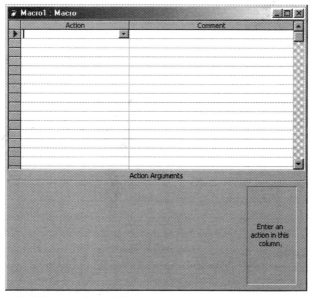.

The **Macro Design** window appears. It is very similar to the **Table Design** window with an upper and lower pane.

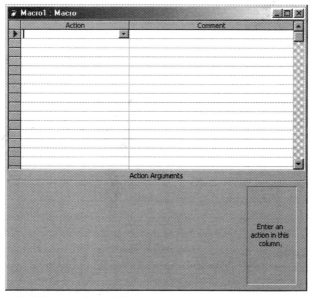

### *Open Publisher detail form* macro

We will deal with the *Publisher detail* form first.

1  In the **Action** column, choose **OpenForm** from the drop-down list of options.

2 Enter a description of what the action will achieve in the **Comment** column. This is optional – it is simply a description of what will happen – you can leave the comment column blank if you wish.

3 In the lower pane, in the **Form Name** field, choose *Publisher detail* form from the drop-down list.

4 Set the data mode to **Edit**.

5 Save your macro. Give it a name that describes what it does – it is easier to remember what a macro does if you name it sensibly.

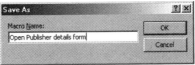

6 Close the **Macro design** window.

Your new macro should be listed under **Macros** in the **Database** window.

### Open the Books grouped by category report macro

This time you will create a new macro that will open your report in Print Preview.

1 Select **OpenReport** as **Action**.

2 The **Report Name** is *Books grouped by category*.

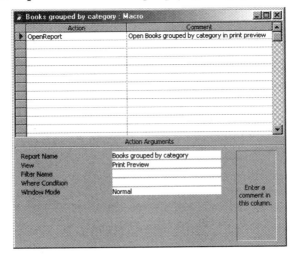

3 Set the **View** to **Print Preview**.

4 Save your macro – you could call it *Books grouped by category*.

5 Close your **Macro design** window.

You should have two macros listed under **Macros** in the **Database** window.

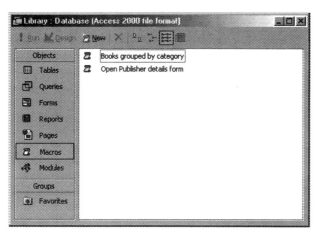

Before going any further, check that your macros work.

# 13.3 Testing a macro

1 Select **Open Publisher details**.

2 Click **Run** Run.

Your publisher detail form should appear on your screen. Close it and test the other macro.

3 Select *Books grouped by category*.

4 Click **Run** Run.

A preview of the report should appear on the screen.

If either of the macros don't work as expected, select the macro and click **Design** to return to **Design** view. Check through the macro specification and fix your error.

# 13.4 Assigning a macro to a button

The next task is to assign these macros to control buttons within the *Book, Author and Publisher details* form.

Once this has been done, you will be able to open the *Publisher details* form and preview the *Books grouped by category* report from within the *Book, Author and Publisher details* form.

1 Take the *Book, Author and Publisher details* form into **Design** view.

2 Scroll to view the **Form Footer** area (resize the area if needed).

The easiest way to get the macros onto your form is to drag them from the Database window and drop them into the Form Footer.

3 Click the **Database window** tool 🖾 (or press [**F11**]) to display the **Database** window.

4 Select **Macros** on the Objects bar in the **Database** window.

You must be able to see both the macro required in the **Database** window and the **Form Footer** area of your form on the screen. Move the **Database** window if necessary.

5 Drag and drop the *Open Publisher details* macro from the **Macros** list to the **Form Footer** area.

6 Display the **Database** window again, and drag and drop the *Books grouped by category* macro into the **Form Footer** area.

In the **Form Design** window, resize the buttons to display the macro name:

7 Select the button.

8 Open the **Format** menu and choose **Size, To Fit**.

Your final design should be similar to the illustration at the top of page 199.

9 Save the changes to your form.

10 Return to Form view.

The control buttons are displayed in the footer area. To run the macro behind the button, simply click the button. Try them out!

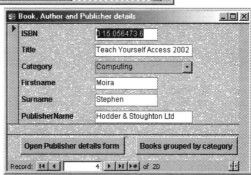

The form with buttons carrying macros, in Design view (top) and Form view (right)

# 13.5 A brief mention of modules

A module is a collection of Visual Basic for Applications declarations and procedures that are stored together as a unit. You can use modules to automate database tasks by using the power and flexibility of the Visual Basic programming language.

Using modules, you can:

• Create event-driven applications (a set of codes that runs when a particular event takes place – perhaps the click of a control button, or data entered into a field).

• Create your own modules (these would be listed on the **Modules** list in the **Database** window).

Or

• Use a custom procedure.

To exploit the facilities offered by the Access Modules object, you really need to be familiar with the Visual Basic programming language.

If you want to learn more about modules, browse the on-line help system. We can only make you aware of them in this Teach Yourself book – not teach you how to write them.

## Summary

Macros and modules are extremely powerful objects. They can be utilized by database developers to automate the way in which Access works. An experienced developer can use them to build very sophisticated databases that can be very easy to use.

In this chapter we have given an introduction to macros and modules. You have learnt how to:

- Create a macro.
- Run a macro.
- Assign a macro to a control button on a form.

**taking it further**

If you've mastered half of what's in this book, you are well on the way to becoming a proficient Excel user. If you are getting to grips with most of it, you are doing very well indeed.

You'll find lots of information on Access on the Internet, in addition to the **Help** menu option **Office on the Web** that takes you to **http://office.microsoft.com/uk/assistance/**.

Other sites that you may find useful include:

**http://www.microsoft.com/office/access /default.asp**

**http://search.support.microsoft.com/search/**

You could also try searching the Web for sites that provide information on Word. Try entering "Microsoft Access" + "Software Reviews" into your search engine. You should come up with several sites worth a look.

If you would like to join a course to consolidate your skills, you could try your local college, or search the Internet for on-line courses. Most courses cost money, but you may find the odd free one – try searching for +Access +Tutorial +Free.

Good Access skills are useful on many different levels – personal, educational and vocational. Now that you have improved your Access skills, why not consider going for certification? The challenge of an exam can be fun, and a recognized certificate may improve your job prospects. There are a number of different bodies that you could consider.

You may want to consider MOUS exams (Microsoft Office User Specialist) or ECDL (the European Computer Driving Licence – basic or advanced) certification. Or, if you feel more ambitious, how about other Microsoft Certified Professional exams!

Visit **www.microsoft.com/traincert/mcp/mous/** for more on MOUS certification or **www.ecdl.com** for information on ECDL.

# appendix: data tables

**Sample data for the Library database tables**

- author
- publisher
- book
- category

# Author table data

| AuthorID | Surname | Firstname | Date of Birth | Date of Death |
|---|---|---|---|---|
| 1 | Peterson | Brian | | |
| 2 | McDonald | Alastair | 12/01/36 | |
| 3 | Jackson | Marion | 24/06/55 | |
| 4 | Adamson | Pauline | | |
| 5 | Duncan | Wilma | 04/07/38 | |
| 6 | Ferguson | John | 03/04/03 | 05/10/88 |
| 7 | Jackson | Allan | 10/12/40 | 02/10/93 |
| 8 | Smith | Dick | | |
| 9 | Schmit | Hans | 12/12/52 | |
| 10 | Camembert | Marion | | |
| 11 | Meunier | Luc | | |
| 12 | Allan | Isabelle | 10/05/65 | |
| 13 | Stephen | Moira | | |
| 14 | MacDonald | Donald | 12/12/20 | 01/03/78 |
| 15 | Williams | Peter | 10/10/30 | |
| 16 | Borthwick | Anne | | |
| 17 | Ferguson | Alan | 04/12/45 | |
| 18 | Wilson | Peter | 12/01/30 | |
| 19 | Smith | Ann | | |
| 20 | Watson | George | 22/10/45 | |

| Nationality | Speciality | Notes |
|---|---|---|
| English | Romantic Fiction | Best seller "Hollywood Days" |
| Scottish | Poetry | |
| English | Travel | |
| Australian | Children's Fiction | |
| American | Travel | |
| Irish | Gardening | |
| Scottish | Travel | |
| Canadian | Children's Fiction | Best seller "The Mounty" |
| German | Computing | PC applications |
| French | Gardening | Best seller "Flowering Shrubs" |
| French | Cooking | |
| Scottish | Travel | |
| Scottish | Computing | PC applications |
| Scottish | Travel | |
| Irish | Science | School textbooks - mainly physics |
| Welsh | Astronomy | TV personality |
| English | Computing | Mainly Computer Science |
| Canadian | Children's Fiction | Famous for "Worst Wizard" books |
| American | Computing | PC applications |
| Austrian | Travel | Writer of TV books |

# Publisher table data

| PublisherID | PublisherName | Address1 | Address2 | City | PostCode |
|---|---|---|---|---|---|
| 1 | Hodder & Stoughton Ltd | 338 Euston Road | | LONDON | NW1 3BH |
| 2 | Borthwick-Henderson | Applewood House | Applewood Hill | OXFORD | O1X1 7DP |
| 3 | Westward Lock Ltd | 18 Clifftop Street | | LONDON | WIX 1RB |
| 4 | Softcell Press | One Softcell Rise | | ORLANDO | 33412-6641 |
| 5 | Christy Corporation | 20 E 103rd Street | | INDIANAPOLIS | 46290 |
| 6 | Arrows Publications | Randall House | 1 Cavalier Bridge Rd | LONDON | SW1V 2SA |
| 7 | Harry Cousin Ltd | 10-23 Frosty Road | South Bank | LONDON | W6 8JB |
| 8 | Beaver Books Ltd | 7 Squirrel Lane | | LONDON | W8 5TZ |
| 9 | Darling Kinghorn Ltd | 2 Herbert Street | | LONDON | WC2E 8PS |
| 10 | City Publications Ltd | 7 Queen Street | | EDINBURGH | EH1 3UG |
| 11 | Scrambler Publications Ltd | 6-9 Prince Street | | LONDON | NW10AE |
| 12 | BPU Publications | Europa House | Queen's Cross | OXFORD | |
| 13 | Outreach College Press | Wilson Way West | | LIVERPOOL | LP3 |
| 14 | Carling & Sons plc | 4 St Thomas' Park | | LONDON | SW1 |
| 15 | Trueform Press Ltd | Manderson House | 8 George Street | LONDON | SW3 6RB |

## Publisher table data (cont.)

| County | Country | Phone Number | Fax Number | E-mail Address | Web Site |
|---|---|---|---|---|---|
| | England | 020 7738 6060 | 020 7738 9926 | jill@hodder.co.uk | Hodder & Stoughton |
| Oxfordshire | England | 01865 333545 | 01865 333444 | bhmarket@repp.co.uk | |
| | England | 020 7333 4454 | 020 7222 4352 | westward.lock@virgin.net | |
| Florida | USA | | | billt@softcell.org.co | |
| | USA | | | marketing@christy.co | |
| | England | 020 7443 9000 | 020 7443 1000 | JoeS@arrows.co.uk | |
| | England | 020 8444 0808 | 020 8444 5000 | Info@harryc.co.uk | |
| | England | 020 7445 7000 | 020 7445 6000 | | |
| | England | 020 8665 7766 | 020 8665 7000 | sales@darkin.co.uk | |
| Midlothian | Scotland | 0131 445 6800 | 0131 445 6236 | scot@citypub.co.uk | |
| | England | 020 8556 4354 | 020 8556 3030 | | |
| Herts | England | | | marketing@bpu.co.uk | |
| | England | | | info@ocp.ac.uk | |
| | | | | karen@carl.co.uk | |
| | England | 020 7334 3344 | 020 7334 2000 | gill@trueform.co.uk | |

# Book table data

| ISBN | Title | AuthorID | PublisherID | CategoryID | Row Number |
|------|-------|----------|-------------|------------|------------|
| 014 032382 3 | In & Out Stories | 8 | 11 | 4 | 3 |
| 0 14 037022 5 | Castaways | 8 | 6 | 4 | 12 |
| 0 14 930654 7 | The 2nd World War | 3 | 14 | 14 | 1 |
| 0 15 056473 6 | Teach Yourself Access 2000 | 13 | 1 | 5 | 12 |
| 0 345 12342 3 | Campfire Cooking | 20 | 8 | 6 | 21 |
| 0 34532 375 1 | Garden Shrubs | 6 | 8 | 11 | 13 |
| 0412 32132 2 | African Drums | 14 | 1 | 1 | 14 |
| 0 412 46512 1 | Bits & Bytes | 13 | 2 | 5 | 12 |
| 0 416 23765 3 | West Highland Way | 7 | 1 | 20 | 14 |
| 0 45 469861 2 | Hamsters at Home | 8 | 6 | 2 | 4 |
| 0 465 77654 3 | Giant World Atlas | 20 | 13 | 20 | 14 |
| 0 482 31456 1 | Easy Internet | 17 | 2 | 5 | 12 |
| 0 55345 456 2 | The Night Sky | 2 | 13 | 3 | 20 |
| 0 563 49124 5 | Bread and Biscuits | 11 | 7 | 6 | 21 |
| 0 576 26111 2 | Crazy Comets | 15 | 13 | 3 | 20 |
| 0 587 39561 0 | Changing Skies | 16 | 2 | 3 | 7 |
| 0 664 58123 4 | Reading with the Under 5's | 8 | 1 | 8 | 6 |
| 0 758 34512 1 | Perfect Pizzas | 11 | 15 | 6 | 21 |
| 0 85234 432 6 | Outdoor Adventures | 12 | 10 | 20 | 14 |
| 0 99988 452 1 | The Tortoise in the Corner | 4 | 6 | 4 | 12 |

# Book table data (cont.)

| Shelf Number | Number of copies | Publication year | Price | Reference | Lending | Picture |
|---|---|---|---|---|---|---|
| 2 | 3 | 1987 | £3.99 | No | Yes | |
| 2 | 2 | 1994 | £4.50 | No | Yes | |
| 5 | 3 | 1988 | £12.50 | No | Yes | |
| 3 | 2 | 2000 | £8.99 | No | Yes | |
| 2 | 1 | 1995 | £4.99 | No | Yes | |
| 2 | 2 | 1986 | £4.99 | No | Yes | |
| 5 | 1 | 1992 | £12.50 | No | Yes | |
| 3 | 2 | 1992 | £9.99 | No | Yes | |
| 4 | 1 | 1992 | £12.50 | No | Yes | |
| 2 | 1 | 1979 | £4.50 | No | Yes | |
| 4 | 1 | 1991 | £35.00 | Yes | No | |
| 2 | 2 | 1996 | £9.99 | No | Yes | |
| 4 | 2 | 1991 | £35.00 | Yes | No | |
| 3 | 2 | 1987 | £12.50 | No | Yes | |
| 3 | 1 | 1989 | £17.50 | No | Yes | |
| 5 | 2 | 1990 | £10.99 | No | Yes | |
| 2 | 2 | 1991 | £6.99 | No | Yes | |
| 5 | 2 | 1986 | £9.99 | No | Yes | |
| 4 | 2 | 1985 | £15.00 | No | Yes | |
| 3 | 2 | 1991 | £6.50 | No | Yes | |

# Category table data

| Category Name |
| --- |
| Adult Fiction |
| Animals |
| Astronomy |
| Children's Fiction |
| Computing |
| Cooking |
| Craft |
| Education |
| Family |
| Foreign Language |
| Gardening |
| Geography |
| Health |
| History |
| Music |
| Poetry |
| Religion |
| Romantic Fiction |
| Science |
| Travel |

# index